PRAYER:
Life's Limitless
Reach

PRAYER:
Life's Limitless Reach

JACK R. TAYLOR

Broadman Press
Nashville, Tennessee

4252-58

ISBN: 0-8054-5258-3

Subject heading: PRAYER
Dewey Decimal Classification: 248.3

Library of Congress Catalog Card Number: 77-073984
Printed in the United States of America

Dedication

To Miss Bertha Smith, prayer warrior and intercessor,
   whose life has left its influence on mine . . .
To Lucy Esch of Denver, Colorado, who faithfully,
   regularly lifts me up to the throne of grace . . .
To Mabel "Grandma" Anderson of Newport News, Virginia,
   who won a lasting place in my heart the first time
   I heard her pray . . .
To Brother W. R. Storie of Jackson, Mississippi, whose life
   is devoted to a ministry of prayer . . .
To those who are best known for prayer and hundreds of
   others who have been intercessors for my ministry
   through the years . . .
To those who aspire to the ministry of intercession and
   are ready to pay the price . . .
To those who are ready to face the fact that of all the
   areas in their lives that of prayer is the neediest
   and are prepared to take measures of repair . . .
I excitedly and expectantly dedicate this volume and issue
   an invitation for you to join me in that realm which
   blasts the boundaries of human limitations . . .

Come with me to
Prayer . . . Life's Limitless Reach

Introduction

"Why another book on prayer?" This is the question that has been revolving in my mind for many months as I have read, surveyed, or browsed more than one hundred volumes on the subject of prayer. It is surely the most journalized subject in Christendom!

Is there some area that has been overlooked that we need to observe in the realm of prayer? I think not! Might there be presented such a simple formula for prayer that thousands could immediately be transformed into praying saints? I doubt it. Is it the fact that of all that has been written there is an inadequate representation of the potential of prayer? Certainly not! Has there been a new discovery on the part of the author that he wishes to set forth? No, for while I may say something new to you, it will not be new in the sense that it has not been said in some manner somewhere before.

"Then why?" I'm glad I asked! I need to hear the answer as I set out to verbalize what is stirring in my heart.

First, there is the fact of an *unexplainable compulsion*. I have allowed this compulsion to bounce against the walls of my soul for more than a year. I protested. Why should a novice venture into such a realm where angels fear to tread? Such supposed audacity delayed me. But the compulsion remained. I will because I must!

Second, there is the fact of a *deepening conviction*. There are times when we reach certain levels of observation that we are prepared to declare an important conclusion. That conclusion seems to rise above all that we have learned and experienced through the years. That conclusion is simply this: The failure of the church is the failure of prayer; the failure of the individual Christian is the failure of prayer! We need look no further! Here is the culprit . . . *prayerlessness!* We have, with all our volumes on it and all our emphasis regarding it, very little real praying today! That conviction has been confirmed again and again as I have been exposed to many levels of Christian activity and enterprise across the world. We may do much that is noble, respectable, and humanitarian, but without prayer it will come to naught!

Third, there is the fact of a *personal discovery*. It is new only in the sense of quality and intensity. I have always known that prayer was the key to the whole relationship with God. But there is knowing and then there is *knowing*. Have you ever known something for years and one day came to discover the riches of what you had known all along? I am discovering a *fulfillment* in prayer that nothing else offers. I am experiencing a *joy* in prayer that no other endeavor provides. I am facing an *excitement* in prayer that time does not dull and no other dimension promises.

I can't imagine a life more exciting than mine on the human plane. Mine is the privilege of meeting God's people across the world and being lovingly accepted and heard by them. World travel is continuously open to me. I never experience monotony! I have more to do that is exciting than I could possibly get done for years. BUT I MUST CANDIDLY CONFESS TO YOU THAT, OF ALL THE EXCITEMENT IN MY LIFE, THE MOST EXCITING AREA IS THAT OF PRAYER. The most priceless privilege that I enjoy is that of meeting God in prayer. I have always known that the potential was there, but I was too busy! I knew that prayer was important, but it was always being shoved into an attendant position . . . that thing we did to get ready for the important thing. If prayer is anything, prayer is everything!

I have never embarked on a task with more expectation and excitement and yet less confidence in my own capacities than are involved in the preparation of this volume. And yet, never has the divine mandate been any more certain.

So come with me to walk over that bridge between two worlds, through that door into another dimension, over that road to life's greatest adventure . . . Come with me to Prayer . . . Life's Limitless Reach!

The author who benefits you most is not the one who tells you something you did not know before, but the one who gives expression to the truth that has been dumbly struggling in you for utterance (Oswald Chambers).

JACK R. TAYLOR, *President*
Dimensions in Christian Living
San Antonio, Texas

Contents

Perspective

This book is designed to leave you praying.

It is not an exhaustive treatise on prayer.

Its purpose is to induce you into the practice of prayer. G. Campbell Morgan has said, "Any discussion of prayer which did not issue in the practice of prayer was not only not helpful but dangerous." We are many and mighty in men and machinery. Yet there is a dearth in vital, victorious, and holy living save for a few places that are notable and joyous exceptions.

There is a power available to the church and the believer of the twentieth century that is virtually untapped, a privilege almost wholly neglected . . . PRAYER! In these days when warnings of waning energy resources are being sounded we need to point to the inexhaustible source of infinite energy open to us through prayer.

We have looked upon prayer as a necessary religious exercise attendant to "matters of greater importance" until we have presented to the world an inferior form of Christianity. We have reduced eternal realities to mere platitudes. The enemy has managed to excite the millions about matters that are meaningless. But the greatest tragedy is that, with eternal truth at our fingertips and the realities of eternity within our grasp, we have managed to tame down the truth and dull the realities. And this we have done to such an extent that we have to invent ways to keep our people interested and attract the world to hear what we have to say!

I have said for years that one of the greatest threats to Christianity is an unexciting Christian. I am not talking about looks, personality, or glamour! I am talking about the excitement that surrounds a person who is living in the realities of another world of unlimited dimensions.

So this is a volume pointing to practice. If it leaves you only impressed and inspired, it has failed! I pray that before you reach past the next few pages you will have the urge to lay the book aside and enter the adventure of prayer. I pray that it will bother you, burden you, and baffle you to prayer.

You will soon discover that the perspective of the book is toward the personal prayer life. This is not to indicate that public prayer or group prayer is unimportant. It is to say that no other kind of prayer will ever be greater than is the nature of the personal prayer life.

There are four points of perspective that I would have you keep in mind as you read:

1. No believer's spiritual life will rise to stay above the level of his praying.

2. No church's ultimate effectiveness will rise to stay above the level of its corporate prayer life.

3. No church's corporate prayer life will be greater than the personal prayer lives of those who make up its constituency.

4. No believer's prayer life will rise to stay above the level of his or her own personal, regular, daily time of worship with God.

Now, I want you to stop right here and read those statements to yourself aloud. I want you to question their veracity. I want you to test their soundness. I had rather you protest them vigorously than to passively consent to their truthfulness. Ask God to confirm them to your heart as you observe your own life and surroundings.

So with this personal, purposeful, and pointed perspective, let's go on!

Part 1
Principles of Prayer

It will be good to note that the book divides itself naturally into three general parts. The first involves principles and precepts in the matter of prayer. The second involves prayer as a personal practice. The third is a series of mini-chapters regarding secrets of prayer.

1

Life's Limitless Reach

Prayer is as illimitable as God's own blessed Son. There is nothing on earth or in heaven, for time or eternity, that God's Son did not secure for us. By prayer God gives us the vast and matchless inheritance which is ours by virtue of his Son. God charges us to "come boldly to the throne of grace." God is glorified and Christ is honored by large asking (E. M. Bounds).[1]

Call unto me, and I will answer thee, and shew thee great and mighty things, which thou knowest not (Jer. 33:3).

The reaches of all of man's faculties are limited—extensive but limited. The strides of science in the past few years have been nothing short of astounding. Our children are observing things with passive nonchalance that would have frightened some of us into becoming runaways in our childhood.

In our generation we have pierced the invisible walls of outer space, landed men on the moon and machines on Mars, and shrunk our world until every continent is only a few hours away. We have created gadgets to make our lives more enjoyable and less laborious. We can tackle mathematical mountains if we can count to ten by the use of a calculator small enough to slip into our shirt pockets or purses!

We can turn a knob with thumb and forefinger and join an event 10,000 miles away with more clarity than those who are there! And promises for more of this are boundless and fulfillment certain if we have time left in history.

"Man's reach is limited, you say?" Yes, write over it all, as astounding as it is . . . limited! Limitation is written over all that man is doing and all that he has done. We are whales in machinery but minnows in morality. Man may seem better *off* but he is not better! We have unlimited media of communication but seemingly nothing profitable to say. We are witnesses to the failure of success!

It should be remembered that God passed by the Roman machinery and the religious hierarchy of 2,000 years ago to bring about the simple happenings in a nameless stable in an unimportant town in the Middle East. All of this was perpetrated by a number of prayer meetings!

I want to reconfirm, "Man's reach, as extensive as it is, is limited!" Even in the realm of extending good, his reach is limited.

A person may move men and women with the vibrance and charisma of his own personality, but his influence is limited to the extensiveness of his presence.

One may speak and be heard by thousands. Through the modern means of amplification and communications, that voice may be heard continents away. That voice, with all its tones and inflections, may be preserved through the years to be heard long after that person is gone. But still the influence is limited. Indeed, take advantage of these means with as much as is in you, but please know—it is limited!

One may write his thoughts on white pages, have them published, and reach the reading eyes of millions. Those writings can be placed in libraries and preserved for centuries. They may even be revived in interest in generations far removed from the days of the author. But this reach is limited!

Man's mind seems near infinity. The thought power of man is fearful. How far can he think? Explosive powers are within the thinking potentials of man. And they tell us that at best we are only using 10 percent of our brain's capacity! But even at that it is limited!

In short, write the word across every human capacity as amazing as the total of them is . . . LIMITED! How tragic for us to settle with the best this world has to give and fail to take advantage of the best God has to give!

But there is a reach that man has been given that is limitless. That reach is prayer! It is as infinite as God for it links the human life to God. It is limitless in space, touching three worlds. It touches heaven, earth, and hell simultaneously and instantaneously. It influences God as no other endeavor. It touches man as nothing else that we can do. It worries the devil more than any human enterprise. The devil hates prayer because it throws the battle to God and pits Him against the enemy with all his resources. Prayer can be launched in an instant and at the speed of thought hits its target! It is not confined to the laws of space.

Prayer knows no limit in time. It belongs to the principles of a transcendent dimension. It can be set off in time, have immediate effect, and reside forever.

God's Invitation to a Limitless Reach

You and I didn't think of prayer. God did! This proposition was not conjured around the council tables of humanity. God said it. "Call unto me, and I will answer thee, and shew thee great and mighty things, which thou knowest not" (Jer. 33:3).

First, look at the *demand*. God says simply, "Call unto me." Everyone can do this, even the speechless. Calling upon God can be done in the mind without the utterance of a word. There is no simpler command made and none more accessible than this. See its *simplicity* . . . CALL! See its *audacity* . . . call *unto me!* Go to the top! Talk to the King! In this offer God invites us, commands us to call upon him! That should send your mind reeling. The God of the universe has condescended to communicate with finite man. He is listening. He hears when you speak! See its *immensity*. He leaves us no condition as to subject matter. We can call upon him regarding anything. The potential subject matter of prayer is infinitely immense. No area of discussion with the father is off limits.

Second, observe the *dynamic*. "And I will answer [you]." Can your mind hold the fact that your praying sends God into action? We can call upon him and his mighty, sovereign will goes into effect. How sickening that we should be content to operate within the confines of our puny power when the power of God is waiting to be released. And the means by which it is released is prayer! I love the sound of that statement, "And I will." God is speaking, friend, and when he says, "I will," you can settle one thing for certain . . . he will!

"And all the inhabitants of the earth are reputed as nothing: and he doeth according to his will in the army of heaven, and among the inhabitants of the earth: and none can stay his hand, or say unto him, What doest thou?" (Dan. 4:35). And it is none other than *this one* who demands that we call upon him; and he declares that he will answer. Observe the designation of his answer. "I will show you." God, as no one else, understands our frame, our density, our infirmities. He knows that it must be simple for us, and he is willing to *show* us!

Third, see the *dimensions*. "Call unto me, and I will answer thee, and shew thee great and mighty things, which thou knowest not." Who can assess the magnitude of these dimensions? We would make God a prisoner in his own universe, disallowing him the prerogative of doing anything outside the boundaries of certain "fixed" laws. We do well to remember who "fixed" them! It is he who says, "I will do great and mighty things." He is not like a mainspring shut within his own works, only acting in one given way. He is not a locomotive keeping to a rigid and appointed iron track, helpless otherwise. We must keep in mind that man's "laws" are interpretations of God's laws which cannot be adequately interpreted! Leave God free to transcend fixed principles. Free him to do great and mighty things!

Pray! Prayer is an invitation to experience the *boundlessness* of God. I am convinced that many folks are not excited about God because they have never discovered his *boundlessness*. Here he has invited us to experience his boundless doing. And his doings doubtlessly will shatter the limitations of your thought power. "I will show you great and mighty things, which you know not!" Aren't you weary with operating within the narrow confines of your understanding? Aren't you tired of being explainable? Prayer opens the door into dimensions beyond understanding.

By all means do as much as you can. Take advantage of all the faculties that are yours. Speak as often and as much of the Lord and his doings as you can. If you are given to writing, put it down for posterity. Extend your influence with all diligence and determination. But with all of this don't neglect the priority of life's limitless reach—that of prayer. Shuck the weights which limit our "goings," being, and "doings" and break through the barrier of our finite limitations and be more than we are, do more than we can do, know more than we know—through the adventure of prayer! Through prayer we can burst this prison of time and space, even while we are here and stand on the shore of eternity and at the foot of the mountain of infinity.

Through this limitless reach we can stand in the NOW and influence the THEN. We can stand in the HERE and touch the THERE. Prayer breaks across the borders of *time* and stands firmly in eternity. It cannot be held in one generation or time slot. Millions of prayers have outlasted the nations and dynasties of their contemporaries and arrived on the shore of another generation safe and sound. Who can tell what prayers now reverberating around the Throne of the universe will be the means of saving our strife-torn, sin-wrecked republic? Yes, and who can tell but that we are now enjoying blessings and mercies because we live in the atmosphere of prayers prayed long ago? No potentate can cancel the efficacy of prayer or lock it within a location or era. No edict can kill its influence.

Look at it! Paul has been dead more than nineteen hundred years and yet, as no theologian or school of thought, he influences Christianity. He is there with Christ because he was *saved*. He is here in influence because he *prayed*. The prayers of Jesus and Paul are surely circling us like celestial sentries guarding their eternal treasures and guiding us through the darkening night of what may well be earth's final century.

Prayer bounds across the borders of the centuries as a runner over hurdles, and prayer shall escort us home. Nothing lies beyond the reach of believing prayer. Past, present, future, time, and space—nothing lies beyond its reach. It is here that the borders of humanity and Deity are breached. Though we are utterly human, when we pray we venture into the realm of the divine. That which is in us, which is more than human, begins to act and interact, and we can touch infinity, God himself.

The early church *exerted* the privilege of prayer. The church of today is in danger of *deserting* the privilege. With all of our technology, inventions, and innovations, let us emphasize, centralize, and "prioritize" on PRAYER—LIFE'S LIMITLESS REACH!

At this moment I must confess to being overwhelmed at what I am thinking. If *grace* is the *river*, prayer is the riverbed through which it flows. If *grace* is the water of life, *prayer* is the pipeline through which it comes. If *grace* is the content, *prayer* is the container from which it is poured. That being true, we cannot separate *grace and prayer*. To speak of one is to speak of the other for we cannot know *grace* apart from *prayer*. Then we could fittingly alter the words of John Newton's hymn to . . .

> Amazing prayer! how sweet the sound,
>   That saved a wretch like me!,
> I once was lost, but now am found,
>   Was blind, but now I see.
>
> Through many dangers, toils, and cares,
>   I have already come;
> 'Twas prayer that brought me safe thus far,
>   And prayer shall lead me home.

---

1. Leonard Ravenhill, *A Treasury of Prayer* (Zachery, La.; Fires of Revival Publishers, 1961), p. 37.

2

The Waiting Miracle

Prayer cures sickness and obtains pardon; it arrests the sun in its course and stays the wheels of the chariot of the moon; it rules over all gods and shuts the storehouses of rain; it unlocks the cabinet of the womb and quenches the violence of fire; it stops the mouths of lions and reconciles our suffering and weak faculties with the violence of persecution; it pleases God and supplies all our need (Jeremy Taylor). [1]

Likewise the Spirit also helpeth our infirmities: for we know not what we should pray for as we ought: but the Spirit itself maketh intercession for us with groanings which cannot be uttered. And he that searcheth the hearts knoweth what is the mind of the Spirit, because he maketh intercession . . . according to the will of God (Rom. 8:26–27).

If we could only know and understand what happens when we pray, we might well have difficulty doing other things that now occupy our main attention. Prayer is a miracle. It has all the credentials of a miracle. Give your favorite definition, and prayer qualifies as a miracle every time. "An earthly event with a heavenly explanation." Prayer passes through that gate with no difficulty. "A happening that is not governed by laws of time and space." Again prayer passes with flying colors. In any description, prayer passes as a miracle.

There has been a recent revival of interest in miracles. Purported miracles have occurred in foreign lands under the auspices of a great spiritual awakening. Christianity seems divided over the feasibility of believing in miracles. Two extreme schools do damage, one refusing to believe in the possibility of miracles and the other demanding a miracle a minute, fabricating one if the genuine doesn't come along. Thousands are waiting for a miracle so they can fully believe. I can with certainty assure you that God is not performing miracles these days to prop up a sagging faith. He has given us his Word for that, and without faith it is impossible to please him.

I believe in miracles! I am a miracle—I am saved! That is the greatest miracle of all. I find no difficulty believing in other types of miracles if I can believe in the greatest miracle of all—salvation! So I suppose that it is good to be waiting for a miracle if the motive is right, faith is in order, and the heart is prepared.

But I want to speak with you about a miracle that is waiting for you! It was waiting for you when you awakened this morning and is waiting for you right now. It will be waiting for you when you go to bed tonight. I call it *the waiting miracle*.

The *waiting miracle* commences with the *problem in the believer*. Our infirmities are the trumpets which call us to prayer. No miracle was performed in the Bible that did not begin in a problem. The 5,000 were fed miraculously because of the problem of hunger. The greater the problem, the greater the solution. Strength was restored to a woman who had the problem of lost health and wealth. The demoniac was healed who was taken with a whole legion of demons. If you don't have a need or a problem, you are not even in the market for a miracle. Let us look at this particular problem in Romans 8:26 ". . . for we know not what we should pray for as we ought." One translation amplifies this: "We do not know what prayers to offer nor how to offer them."

Thus the problem in the believer is twofold. First, he has the problem of *ignorance*. He neither knows what to pray for or how to pray. Now that is no small problem. If we pray on the basis of knowledge of the human side, we will miss the heart of our real need. The symptom will distract us from the problem, and we will pray amiss. Second, there is the problem of *impotence*. The word in the Greek is *asthenos* for "infirmities." "The Spirit helps our infirmities." The word literally means "strengthless," being *sthenos* (strength) with a negative prefix. W. E. Vine says that it means the negative of strength, indicating the inability to produce results. No words could better describe us! We are on the one hand weak, strengthless, helpless, *impotent,* and on the other hand *ignorant* in regard to what we really need and how to pray.

This is what you would call a total problem! This is the place the waiting miracle begins. We would not pray if we had no need. God both allows and engineers our situations of need so that we might pray. The miracle has been waiting all the while. Only with the emergence of the need was the miracle in prospect. This is where help comes. Better still, this is where the *Helper* comes.

The waiting miracle continues with the *partnership of the Spirit.* "The Spirit *helps* our infirmities." Now, I want you to see this, the most profound issue in this statement, "The Spirit *helps.*" The implication is that prayer is a double harness, a dual responsibility. God brings about the need in our lives and we decide to pray. When we do, the Spirit *helps* us. The word in Greek is a tongue twister, *sunantilambanomai.* This literally means "to lay hold along with, to take hold with another."

Let us clarify with two illustrations. First, there is a large log to be carried, too heavy and too long for one man. He picks up one end of it, and another takes hold of the other end (*sunantilambanomai*). Prayer is too weighty for a mere human. He cannot bear it alone. The Spirit of God takes hold of the other end and helps us pray! Hallelujah! Next, there is the illustration of a team of horses. There are dual harnesses. One horse gets into harness, but he cannot go. The burden of the base is too great, and the harness is for two. Another horse gets into the other harness. I take up the task of prayer, but alas it's too weighty. It wasn't made to be borne alone. It is then that the Holy Spirit *helps* (sunantilambanomai) our infirmities picking up on the other end of this affair, and we pray under the control of the Spirit.

The Holy Spirit, indispensable in the endeavor of prayer, first *intercedes.* Notice the nature of his intercession. It is *personal* intercession "for us." The Holy Spirit is a personal intercessor, specific in the nature of his intercession. Again, it is *prevailing* intercession. "With groanings which cannot be uttered." The picture

here is one of urgent supplication. He not only intercedes personally
and prevailingly but *purposefully*. His intercession is *"according to
the will of God"* (v. 27). That is prayer which joins itself to life's
highest purpose known only to God.

The Spirit not only intercedes—he *intervenes*. If he prays for us
according to the will of God, then, helping our ignorance, he heads
us off from praying the wrong prayers. I have written in my Bible
over Romans 8 these words: "We are so weak, so ignorant, and so
blind that did not God in his mercy withhold what we ask, we should
be ruined by our own request."

It is as if the Holy Spirit runs a clearing house for our prayers.
Knowing the mind of the Father, he bends our praying to that which
is according to God. (The term *the will of* is in italics and is not in the
original text.)

Paul reminded the Corinthians they were temples of the Holy
Spirit which dwelt in them. The purpose of a temple is worship. We
are the means of the Holy Spirit's worshiping in us. Prayer is
worship. We are partners with the Holy Spirit in the venture of
prayer.

The waiting miracle consummates in the purpose of the Father.
The word *and* in verse 28 connects the Scripture we have read with
that which follows. It is in missing this little word that many stand
mistaken as to what verse 28 implies. It is only within the context of
the prayer relationship that all things work together for good and only
within the relationship that we know it. Let's read the Scripture.
"And we know that all things work together for good to them that
love God, to them who are the called according to his purpose. For
whom he did foreknow, he also did predestinate to be conformed to
the image of his Son, that he might be the firstborn among many
brethren. Moreover whom he did predestinate, them he also called:
and whom he called, them he also justified: and whom he justified,
them he also glorified" (vv. 28–30).

We shall miss the main point of this passage if we do not repeat it.
It is: that the purpose of God is achieved in the prayer relationship.
We are weak and ignorant. The Holy Spirit takes up the matter of our
weakness and prays with us that we might fit into the purpose of
God. In this latter passage, the purpose of the Father is clarified and
the manner in which it is achieved is equally as clear. We shall not

know that all things work together for good apart from the partnership of the Spirit in the venture of prayer. It is out of such a relationship that we know confidently that whatever happens will all cooperate for good to those who love God.

I want you to see three things relative to the purpose of the Father. First, there is the fact of *determined providence*. Only a God who is absolutely sovereign could allow such a claim to be made of him. Nothing can happen but that he fits it together in his all-inclusive providence to fit his final design. What a marvelous fact! What a delicious truth! Think of it, all things energize together for good! All things! Second, there is the fact of a *designated people*. It is not true in the life of the heathen. He cannot lay hold of this fact. This is a promise to a conditioned people—to those who love God and are the called according to his purpose. But, alas, added to a determined providence that assures the cooperation of all things to God's purpose, and a designated people destined to achieve that purpose, there is a *definite program* which guarantees consummation.

God has worked all of this out ahead of time. He has left nothing out—not one single detail. What a comfort to know that from God's standpoint the process is completed. I have only to reckon real by faith what is already real to live in the victory of an already-accomplished purpose. Praise the Lord! Look at the process! It is significant that all these words are in the past tense (Greek aorist). The tense guarantees accomplishment, not on the basis of hope but on the basis of certainty. It is now! He foreknew. Whom he foreknew (knew beforehand), he predestinated (predetermined). The "whom" designates everybody he started with in the redemption process. He lost no "whoms" along the way! All he predetermined, he called. All he called, he justified, that is, restored to his favor, declaring not guilty. But the most amazing thing is that he glorified all of these whom he has foreknown, predestinated, called and justified. No wonder that we are enjoined by Jesus in Mark 11:22 to have the faith of God which is the (literal interpretation of the statement, "Have faith in God"). God's faith declares that our redemption is already complete and indeed from his viewpoint it is. As we live the prayer life, we are in touch with God's viewpoint and from that vantage point we live on the grounds of redemption. It is only when we lose the advantage of his viewpoint that our situation becomes grave.

When I am determined to keep his view of me over against my view of me, I am on victory terms with life.

Thus we have a determined providence, a designated people, and a definite program. And all that completed!

What shall we *then* say? What shall we say *when?* When we through the waiting miracle of prayer find ourselves helped by the Spirit in the achievement of the purpose of the Father. That is *when!* The glad knowledge of all these delightful facts leads us to say, "If God be for us, who can be against us?" (Rom. 8:31). The literal Greek is interesting here. It can be read, "If the God for us, who against us?" And who indeed? God has thought of everything. That leaves nothing to chance, fate, or the enemy. No one in heaven can be against us, for his throne is set in the heavens. No one on earth, for the earth is the Lord's and the fullness thereof. No one in hell for the accusations of the enemy are buried in the blood of Jesus.

Now, let me say it again. There is a miracle which waits for you. It is there all the time. No appointment is needed prior to it. No special qualification need be awaited. There are no office hours or time limits. That waiting miracle is prayer. It begins with the *problem of the believer*—one of impotence and ignorance. It continues with the *partnership of the Spirit*, who both intercedes and intervenes according to the will of God. It climaxes in the *purpose of the Father*, his determined providence, his designated people, and his definite program.

Prayer is that waiting miracle. You are waiting for a miracle? A miracle is waiting for you! "Stand up, stand up for Jesus, The strife will not be long; This day, the noise of battle, The next, the victor's song!"

---

1. *Ibid.*, p. 60.

3

Jabez . . . an Example in Prayer

The potency of prayer hath subdued the strength of fire; it hath bridled the rage of lions, hushed anarchy to rest, extinguished wars, appeased the elements, expelled demons, burst the chains of death, expanded the gates of heaven, assuaged diseases, repelled frauds, rescued cities from destruction, stayed the sun in its course, and arrested the progress of the thunderbolt. Prayer is an all-sufficient panoply, a treasure undiminished, a mine which is never exhausted, a sky unobscured by clouds, a heaven unruffled by storm. It is the root, the fountain, the mother of a thousand blessings (Chrysostom). [1]

And Jabez was more honourable than his brethren: and his mother called his name Jabez, saying, Because I bare him with sorrow. And Jabez called on the God of Israel, saying, Oh that thou wouldest bless me indeed, and enlarge my coast, and that thine hand might be with me, and that thou wouldest keep me from evil, that it may not grieve me! And God granted him that which he requested (1 Chron. 4:9–10).

Here is one of the most unique passages of Scripture in the entire Bible! Here is a man almost nobody knows! I have asked across the country who has ever heard of Jabez and only on occasion is there anyone who has. His name is tucked away amid a myriad of other names, above five hundred in all, in the first chapters of 1 Chronicles. What a blessing came to me the first day I was introduced to

27

him. And many have been the blessings since. He is a prime example
of prayer for us.

Our gliding through the Bible rather passively is apt to cause us to
miss Jabez. There are whole stretches of Scripture where names
appear with no historical reference or one distinguishing fact. They
glide on stage and off without one characteristic to mark their
appearance. Most of them are never mentioned again, and we know
little or absolutely nothing about them. But in 1 Chronicles: 4 there is
an abrupt change with verse 9. Out of all the previously mentioned
names, that of Jabez demands attention. The divinely appointed and
anointed biographer is impelled to explain this man above all others.
Thus we have almost hidden away in a raft of other names that of
Jabez, the man known by few whose example should be followed by
all. His biography occupies less than eighty words in the English
text, and yet it speaks volumes to us today which, if heeded, would
change our lives and our world.

What facts we have regarding Jabez are clear and concise. They
are stated but not enlarged upon as if no further explanation is
needed. He is abruptly and briefly introduced and just as abruptly
dismissed, not to be mentioned again. The only other thing that I
have been able to find is that there was a city by that same name.

We know nothing of the properties he owned, the public offices he
might have held, the family he might have had, or the deeds he did,
except the one thing for which he is known. But what we do know
about him is enough to change our life-styles and to usher us into a
new age of usefulness and fulfillment.

First, let us observe the prominence that described him.

He was more honorable than his brethren. That is the terse manner
in which he is introduced. Above the hundreds before him who did
nothing worthy of mention, he was more honorable. Our attention is
arrested at once by such a description. For there is a drive within
each of us to achieve, to succeed, to excel. We are interested in any
secret of a person's success and excellence. We don't have to achieve
prominence on God's scale, but we should ever live with the desire
and the demand both from without and within. The example of Jabez
calls us from the sickening sameness of our age where the dare to be
different has been dulled by the curse of conformity. The insights of
individuality are dumped into the pool of collective ignorance and

become the accepted consensus.

Jabez was not such a one. He refused to be stereotyped and broke with the crowd. It can never be said of someone determined to be "one of the fellows" that he was more honorable than his brethren. To be more honorable, one must be alone, but he is alone out front! King Jehoshaphat asked in 1 Kings 22:7, "Is there not here a prophet of the Lord *besides*, that we might enquire of him?" Vance Havner suggests that it is hard to be a prophet *besides*. It is difficult to be the exception, not to be part of the accepted group, the "in" crowd. But we should be reminded that eagles do not fly in flocks or formations. They do not depend on the safety of numbers for their existence. Geese fly in flocks and ducks in formation. I suppose it all depends on whether you want to go through life honking or quacking in unison with the establishment or soaring in the heavenlies with God!

It matters a great deal to your age and mine how we shall be described. We sometimes pay a high price to be "one of the boys." Woe to the preacher who mixes with his people to the point that they say, intending to compliment, "Oh, he is just one of us!"

Where there is no vision the people perish. Visions of the nation-saving kind are not arrived at in committee or group discussions or dialogues. They come from singular men more honorable than their brethren—men or women whose attention has been arrested by a lingering gaze upon God.

Jabez was more honorable than his brethren!

Second, let us observe the pain that designated him. "His mother called his name Jabez, saying Because I bare him with sorrow." This presents a mystery we shall not solve on this side of eternity. What a strange title to live under. Now I have known some people in my time for whom the name "Pain" would seem rather fitting! But what a name to be handed at birth! We do not know whether his mother had great difficulty in bearing him or whether he was born a cripple with a painful defect to carry through life. Pain may have been his roommate for the length of his life.

Regardless of the reason for this designation, the thing we should take notice of is that *pain* and *prominence* go together. Have you noticed the frequency with which we find these two living at the same address? How often *hurting* makes us prominent *helpers*. You might as well make up your mind that if you would achieve promi-

nence in the things of the Lord you will be on speaking terms with
pain and trouble. Our Savior was one who was called a man of
sorrows and acquainted with grief! If we are going to be redemptive,
we shall walk the same paths. Difficulty was no stranger to Paul nor
has any determined Christian ever become exempt from tribulation.
Paul went around confirming the souls of the disciples "exhorting
them to continue in the faith, and that we must through much
tribulation enter into the kingdom of God" (Acts 14:22).

But the central issue in Jabez's case is the praying that distinguished him.

"And Jabez called upon the God of Israel. . . ." Now don't pass
over this too quickly. This is rather amazing. A man is known for
what he does the most. If he does not do much of anything, he is
known for nothing. And if a man is to achieve notice in any given
area, he must do more of it than anyone else. A man will never be
designated as a man who loves God who seems to love him less than
others. His love must exceed that of others. Jabez called on God—he
prayed.

Notice the *certainty* of his praying. If a man prays some, he will
perhaps be noticed. To be honored for it, he must pray much. As we
read this brief biography, we catch a note of concluding finality. He
prayed! It is as simple as that! He was prominent because he prayed.
There need be no other reason. He prayed!

Notice the *consistency* of his praying. The implication is easy to
see. That he prayed was important. That he prayed much and regularly is monumental. The construction is such as to suggest that he
called, and called upon the God of Israel until he was recognized as
one who always prayed.

Notice the *content* of his praying. It is vital that he prayed. It is
more vital that he prayed regularly and consistently. It is even more
vital that he prayed so consistently the same prayer that we have
recorded the precise content of it. That we know he prayed is *good*.
That we know *what* he prayed is *glorious*. Let us examine the basic
design of his prayer. It falls rather naturally into four parts:

Oh that thou wouldest bless me indeed

There are three things that can be noticed right away from the
sound of these words. First, it was *urgent*. You can't read that prayer
and make it sound right by reading it casually. There is a note of

urgency about it. "Oh, that thou wouldest bless me indeed . . ."
Second, it was *personal*. Now that is audacious. How often in mock
humility are we prone to shun a prayer like that. Not Jabez! He was
bold in asking for a personal blessing. No false humility here! "Oh
that you would bless ME!" Finally, it was *daring*. The word indeed
is a word of quality. He was not asking for something small. It is one
thing to have a blessing, quite another to be blessed INDEED! It is one
thing to have life, quite another to have life INDEED! How much we
are kept from blessings because we fail to pray for the INDEED, the
excellent, the extraordinary!

. . . AND enlarge my coast

A man's border or coast marks the limit of his influence. His coast
denotes the realm of his responsibility. Jabez was praying for ex-
tended responsibility, lengthened influence, heightened opportunity.
He unapologetically was asking for more real estate, more influence,
and more life. One of the certain signs of divine life is the desire for
the much more! I trust that you are desirous of a blessing as was
Jabez. Don't ever apologize for that fact, and don't ever leave
without the desired blessing. If you and I are blessed from the hand
of God, others will be blessed through our blessedness. But how
often is this desired blessedness brought about through distress!
David declared, "Thou hast enlarged me when I was in distress"
(Ps. 4:1) A man's borders are often stretched through the continuing
pain of distasteful circumstances that would be avoided if possible.
The psalmist said again, "I called upon the Lord in distress: the Lord
answered me, and set me in a large place" (118:5).

This may well be the boldest prayer ever prayed by a common
man. It pulsates with unvarnished audacity. And, if we did not know
the outcome, we might suspect that the prayer was too selfish to be
answered.

And that thine hand might be with me

Jabez surely is wise enough to know that it would be a mistake to
have the blessing of God without the hand of God along with it.
More have been ruined from too much blessing than by too much
distress. With God's blessings comes his hand. Blessedness is the
greatest of perils. It tends to dull our keen sense of dependence on
God and make us prone to presumption. God cannot trust us with
great blessing without his hand to guide us through the very perils of

it. "Put your hand upon me, Lord!" Jabez was giving God an open hand with his life. He was asking to be controlled, directed, taken over by the hand of the Lord.

> . . . And that you wouldest keep me from evil,
> that it might not grieve me!

The final petition was important. Does a man have the right to pray that no evil will befall him? I think that this is not the issue here. He is praying that he might be kept from evil, not evil kept from him. Jesus taught us to pray, "Deliver us from evil." But he was not praying that we might be exempt from exposure. We are to experience victory over evil. Jabez was praying, "Keep me from the evil effects of evil in my own life." We cannot be kept from the exposure to evil, but we can be delivered from the evil effects of evil. He did not want to be grieved by his own actions.

So we have the content of his praying. The casual reader might be prone to say, "What a perfectly selfish prayer!" But before you embarrass yourself with such a verdict, read the concluding statement—"And God granted him that which he requested!"

Notice, finally, the preference that delighted him.

The life story of Jabez was as simple as that. He knew what he wanted and went for it. He knew where and to whom to go for it; he asked for it; and he received it!

Does God have favorites and practice preference? In a manner he does. He *prefers* to answer those who ask him! The writer of Proverbs tells us that God is delighted with prayers of the righteous (15:8). He shows great and mighty things to them who call upon him (Jer. 33:3). There are people who seemingly get everything they want. They have learned the simple secret that if they delight in the Lord he will give them the desires of their hearts (Ps. 37:4).

The curtains close upon Jabez with these words: "And God granted him that which he requested!"

I come to suggest to you that here is an example that we do well not to avoid. Here is one on whom was conferred a high degree because of something which we are almost totally neglecting— namely, the life of prayer. We are in desperate need of a return to personal and prevailing prayer. We shall not be saved from our spiritual doldrums by more programs and better strategy. God's chief method has always been people and prayer!

Praying for the right thing and getting it is success pure and simple. It is not working for God but seeking God to the extent that God is able to work on his own behalf inside us in our surroundings.

I believe that of all the facts which we are called upon to believe, this is the most profound—that God can still move through the sheer power of prayer to unseat the enemy, relocate the saints in positions of victory and triumph, and deliver his causes to success. In this day when *big* is *beautiful* and *huge* is *holy*, we are called upon to declare that through prayer God can "thresh a mountain with a worm," and the lame can take the prey. God has always bypassed bigness in favor of devoted praying. A prophet like Elijah with no credentials in big government locked the heavens with his praying and opened them again, holding sway over the economy of the whole country! If we could only believe again that prayer is our priority! If we could but realize that one man meeting with God can wield more influence than a marching army, we would go to prayer!

But we have orphaned prayer to an inferior position, neither greatly berated nor greatly respected.

Now, take a few minutes to read aloud 1 Chronicles 4:9–10 several times. Receive Jabez as a permanent friend. Repeat his prayer often. Follow his example much

1. *Ibid.*, p. 22.

4

The Problem of Prayerlessness

Non-praying is lawless, discord, anarchy. The whole force of Bible statement is to increase our faith in the doctrine that prayer effects God, secures favor from God, which can be secured in no other way, and which will not be bestowed if we do not pray (E. M. Bounds).[1]

God forbid that I should sin against the Lord in ceasing to pray for you (1 Sam. 12:23).

I have stated earlier that no believer's spiritual life will ever rise to stay above the level of his or her praying. Because this is true, we should begin to investigate at this point when there is failure in the church or in the individual Christian life. I am convinced that the failure of the church is the failure in prayer. Likewise the failure of the Christian is the failure in prayer. Prayer touches all that we are if it touches us at all. The weakness of our serving, loving, and giving may be but a symptom of the failure in prayer. S. D. Gordon said, "If a man be right and put the practice of praying in the right place, then his speaking, serving, and giving will be fairly fragrant with the presence of God."

I think that it will not do much good just to score the sin of prayerlessness though I certainly do want to mark the sinfulness of it. I have had the experience of hearing about someone who had a great life of prayer. While it *impressed* me, it also *depressed* me. For while I deeply desired to have that sort of prayer life, I would

34

remember the dozens of times I would struggle to get out of routines in which prayer was not a priority. The struggle would last a few days or a few weeks at the most, and I would be right back where I was before. It did not seem to help me to be told that I must pray more. I already knew that. Someone needed to take me past that point of recognition and repentance to show me how to achieve the position of prayer. I have said this to caution you from turning away from this chapter with feelings of guilt. This could be the most important chapter you will read. We are going to deal with prayerlessness as a *sin*, as a *stronghold*, and as a *defeat*. While there are overlapping areas of truth in these, I have found it very helpful to deal with them as separate areas. The truths we are about to observe have liberated hundreds of folks to a new level of prayer.

A Definition of Prayerlessness

We should come to a workable definition of what we mean by prayerlessness. Perhaps there are few who don't pray at all, and I hope very few. I am inclined to believe that a person who prays not at all needs to be saved. I am very doubtful of the possibility that a person could have the praying person of the Holy Spirit living in him or her without praying some.

Prayerlessness, for our consideration here, could be defined as *that state in which one prays less than he ought, less than the Father desires, and less than that one himself knows he should.* Now I know that that definition cuts such a swath that we all are included, and for this consideration that is good! Who among the readers of this volume has escaped the perils of prayerlessness? Isn't it true that you could, if you would be candidly honest, trace most of your failure to one root—prayerlessness?

Prayerlessness as a Sin

Prayerlessness is a sin! Not just a weakness! If we look upon it as a weakness, we will attempt to strengthen ourselves in that area, but to no avail. A sin can only be dealt with by repentance, confession, forgiveness, and cleansing. But before continuing with that, I want you to see just how serious is the sin of prayerlessness.

Prayerlessness is a sin against the *person* of God. God has commanded us to pray, told us that he delighted in the praying of the righteous, and left us certain instructions. In the light of these facts, prayerlessness is lawless anarchy against the person of God.

Prayerlessness is a sin against the *purpose and plan* of God. All that God does, he does through prayer. Everything that has come to man has come through the agency of prayer. God has given us prayer as the one agency by which we can get heaven down to earth. Jesus taught us to pray, "Thy kingdom come, Thy will be done in earth, as it is in heaven." It is not only the means of implementation in the kingdom, but it is the means of implementation of all the principles of the individual life of the believer. To neglect prayer as a priority is treason against the proposals of God. And what is more audacious is that the sin is always compounded by the fact that once we neglect it, we must install our own flesh-born programs in its place.

Prayerlessness is a sin against the *pleasure* of God. Someone has said that prayer means infinitely more to God than it does to man. I am sure that is true as far as the consciousness of the value of it is concerned. The point I want to make here is that prayer is a *pleasure* to God. Proverbs 15:8 tells us, "The prayer of the upright is his delight." Now that is profound to me! God enjoys my praying! The hours of joy, aside from all that they benefit me, bring joy to the Father.

This was brought out to me several years ago when I announced to my family that I would begin to rise very early in the morning to meet the Lord. My daughter, Tammy, said, "Dad, would you wake me up when you get up?" I replied that I would be glad to and inquired why she desired to be awakened. Her reply was that she wanted to join me in the experience of prayer. I cannot describe the pleasure that welled up within my soul. I carried that through the day, and as I went to bed that night I had a sense of deep anticipation. I thought within myself, "Now, why am I so joyous on the inside?" The answer came quickly. My daughter would meet me at the throne of grace, and we would pray together.

God reminded me that all my feelings of love and pleasure concerning my children came from him. If I found pleasure in praying with my offspring, how much more joy does the Father get from praying with his own? An obedient child desires to bring pleasure to the heart of the father. So with a child of God. Prayerlessness is an affront to the joy of the Father.

Prayerlessness is a sin against the *promises* of God. The Bible is packed with prayer promises. When a promise is made, the one to whom it is made is under obligation to take advantage of it. He cannot be neutral and act as if he never heard. He is obliged to live in the benefits of it. When he does not, there is a breach against the promise which is ignored. "Ye have not because ye ask not" is a charge that can be leveled against any of us when we allow ourselves to remain in a situation from which we could be delivered by prayer.

Prayerlessness is a sin against the *power* of God. All of God's mighty power is available to the church and the Christian of the twentieth century. The channel through which that power comes to us is prayer. To seek or prefer another means of doing what God has assigned us to do is sheer insubordination to God's power.

Now, are you convinced that prayerlessness is a sin? Then don't wait to confess it candidly, repent right now, and receive the glad forgiveness of the Father along with cleansing. Don't wait to do that. Do it right now! The remaining chapters will be a delight if you will. "Lord, I own up to the sin of praying too little; of praying less than I know I ought, less than I know you desire of me, and less than I really want to. I ask you to not only forgive me but also preside over this experience of becoming a prayer warrior. Open my heart to any truths that may mean deliverance to prayerfulness."

Prayerlessness as a Stronghold

It is at this point that we may be moving into some new territory for you. It was for me until a short while ago. I came to it because of despair over the problem of prayerlessness. How I wrestled with the problem! I would come to guilt, confess, receive forgiveness, and go right back into the same pattern. I would fight the early morning battle for several straight days and one morning roll over and go back to sleep and from there on it would be downhill—the wrong way.

I happened to be in Southeast Asia ministering to the missionaries. One night I spoke to them on the necessity of much prayer and the Lord put me under conviction anew. I went back to my room early that evening and got on my knees and said something like this to the Lord: "Father, I have been here over and over again. I have asked you dozens of times to forgive me of the sin of prayerlessness and I know you have. But I don't want to have to come again and again seeking forgiveness from the same sin. Now is there anything I need to know about what is happening or what needs to happen in my life as far as prayer is concerned?'' Well, the Lord sent an answer to my heart immediately.

Prayerlessness, like most other sins, is more than a sin if it is allowed to exist across the years. It develops into a *stronghold*. Let me use a personal illustration to show you what I mean. I was not schooled in the importance of prayer when I was a very young Christian. Somehow I remember *knowing* that it was important anyway. Thus, early in my Christian life I developed much in prayer. As a lad my place of private prayer was the cellar—the warmest place in the winter and the coolest place in the summer. How I prayed and with what delight!

But as the years came on and business increased with college, marriage, and seminary, I found the battle to pray increasing in intensity. It was always the lessons, the work, the television, and other things that took me from the place of prayer. Now, to be sure the prayerlessness was a sin but it would become more than a sin. I developed an aversion to getting up early. My body told me that there was bound to be a better way of beginning the day than getting up! How I loved the hours of sleep just before dawn. It became a fixation to me. I would often even set the alarm two hours before I wanted to get up so I would enjoy the consciousness of going back to sleep for those two extra hours. The pleasure of other things became brighter than the experiences in prayer. When at intervals, I did rise early to try to pray, I seemed not to be able to get with it. That failure was added to the memory bank to be used later as ammunition for the enemy in thwarting my praying.

Well, that night in Southeast Asia on my knees, God revealed to me that the enemy had built up a stronghold in my life. The words of Paul came to me, having become precious to me previously, ''The weapons of our warfare are not carnal, but mighty through God to the pulling down of strong holds; Casting down imaginations, and every high thing that exalteth itself against the knowledge of God, and bringing into captivity every thought to the obedience of Christ'' (2 Cor. 10:4–5). I realized that though I had been to God many times with the confession of my prayerlessness, I had never faced the problem as one of a stronghold.

I saw that the stronghold involved my thought processes, my body metabolism, my preferences, and my decision-making faculties. I brought myself to the Lord on such a plane as I had never been conscious before for whatever divine operation he desired to perform in me.

As I understood the weapons of this warfare, I employed them in Jesus' name against the stronghold I had allowed the enemy to build up in my life. The Word of God, the blood of Christ (the emblem of his finished work on the cross), the name of Jesus Christ (the emblem of all that he is), the testimony of my faith in Jesus Christ, and a commitment of loyalty to the death—these were among the entities that I considered the "weapons." (In Rev. 12:11 we read, "And they overcame him by the blood of the Lamb, and by the word of their testimony; and they loved not their lives unto the death.")

As I stood against the stronghold, by faith I counted the transaction done! I accepted my deliverance from the limitations that had been imposed by my disobedience and maintained by the power of the enemy. I testify to you that it happened. I have not been the same since. I am not testifying that it has been a matter of perfection but it has been decidedly different.

The first thing that happened was that my mind was clear to decide to make prayer vital in my own life and schedule. The next thing that happened was that I awakened the next morning early and unhindered to spend time with the Lord. This may be of help to you. You may have been struggling for years with the problem and have almost given up in disgust and disappointment. *God is still mighty to the pulling down of strongholds!*

Notice what else happens as the strongholds fall. Imaginations are cast down. High things are put down. Every thought is brought into captivity to the Lord Jesus Christ. Imagine that! If that could happen to your life right now, you would be prepared to pray! Why not just pray something like this:

Lord, I come to you with the problem of prayerlessness. I ask you to forgive me, confessing it as a sin, and I am glad to receive my forgiveness. Thank you very much!

Now, Lord, I desire you to clean out every hindrance to my prayer life. I stand against anything that the enemy has imposed upon me through my disobedience. I stand against laziness, preoccupation, time-wasting, sleepiness, and any other thing that keeps me from prayer. I close every door I have ever opened to the enemy; I break every agreement I have ever made with him through my disobedience; I take back every parcel of ground I have ever given him in my life; I refuse him any place in me and any power over me. I am God's property. My body is a temple of the Holy Spirit who lives in me right now. I claim every stronghold pulled down, every imagination cast down, every high thing put down, and every thought captured by Jesus Christ. I accept the fact of my deliverance from the stronghold of prayerlessness right now by faith. Thank you Lord!

Now, spend a few minutes thanking God for his mighty power to the pulling down of strongholds. "Stand fast therefore in the liberty wherewith Christ has made us free, and be not entangled again with the yoke of bondage" (Gal. 5:1). As delightful as this is, it is not all our consideration in the matter of the problem of prayerlessness.

Prayerlessness as Defeat

For my sin, I have forgiveness; for the stronghold, I have deliverance; for my defeat in prayer, I have the prayer life of JESUS in me for my victory in prayer. I will not cover all here that might be covered. I will deal with it later under the discussion of the name of Jesus. It is enough to say here that Jesus left us his prayer life and all its vitality as he left us his name. He lives within us to be all that God requires and all that we desire. He is my life. He is my loving life, my serving life, my giving life, and my praying life! It is by laying hold of the life of Christ in me that I can learn to pray. As the Holy Spirit takes the things of Christ as is promised of him, the prayer capacities of Jesus begin to become real in me! His life is one of victory and he is mine—both in life and victory!

Take a moment now to review the chapter. Allow God to deal with you even in those areas where you are not intellectually certain. Submit your prayer life as it is to the Lord and to whatever cleansing and deliverance he desires to do in you. Accept the triumphant praying life of Jesus in you as your hope of glory in prayer. Begin now to allow him to shape your prayer life according to his life in you. Remember, prayer is your life's limitless reach! Begin to use it to the glory of God.

1. *Ibid.*, p. 23.

5

What Is Prayer, Anyway?

Prayer is our need crying out for help.
Prayer is the voice of faith to the Father.
Prayer is the Living Word in lips of faith (E. W. Kenyon.)
Prayer is the channel through which all good flows from God to man, and all good from men to men. Prayer is a privilege, a sacred, princely privilege. Prayer is a duty, an obligation most binding, and most imperative, which should hold us to it. But prayer is more than a privilege, more than a duty. It is a means, an instrument, a condition. It is the appointed condition of getting God's aid. It is the avenue through which God supplies man's wants (E. M. Bounds).[1]

It is time to ask the question, "What is prayer anyway?" But why now, why this late in the book? I have an idea that we are not really ready for the answer to that question until we are convinced of the importance of prayer in the first place.

I have already said that prayer looks out on three worlds. We shall deal with the nature of prayer from this vantage point. We will discuss prayer as *worship;* prayer as *work;* prayer as *warfare.*

Prayer as Worship

We should be reminded that prayer is not just a means of getting things from God but is the means whereby we may come to *know* God. Prayer, in its primary essence, is worship. Worship is the recognition of worth, the fitting of God into the overall picture of our lives in his proper perspective. The very act of prayer, whether we kneel, sit, lie on our faces, or stand is an affirmation of the worthiness of God.

Without prayer there is no worship. Armin R. Gesswein, in his splendid booklet, *Seven Wonders of Prayer*, says, "By prayer we enter into God's holy temple, and penetrate at once to the throne of grace. Prayer is not only the shortest distance to God's mighty throne, it is the only way in. To think that this supreme wonder could take place so suddenly with one bold, blood-bought step! There we see the Lord Jesus ever living to pray for us, and ready to give us of His own praying by His Spirit. Glorious discovery: He is only a prayer away! The veil of sense and space that hides Him within His temple-universe is suddenly removed as we pray. We enter silently into His temple, and lo, suddenly we are before His throne. Priests, before our great High Priest. There too, we are suddenly in the presence of angels and archangels, and with all the company of Heaven we worship and adore Him. Only there do we discover the wonder of worship, that worship is before work, and that all His works are done in the spirit of worship. There are many churchgoers, but few worshipers, because there are few 'pray-ers.' " [2]

So as prayer looks toward God, it is *worship*. This is its primary essence. There are only two ways by which we can get to know God—through his Word and through prayer. But the fact is that while the Word contains facts about God, only through prayer and prayerful use of the Word can we use it to get to know God.

Prayer as Work

"Verily, verily, I say unto you, He that believeth on me, the works that I do shall he do also; and greater works than these; . . . because I go to my Father. And whatsoever ye shall ask in my name, that will I do, that the Father may be glorified in the Son. If ye shall ask any thing in my name, I will do it" (John 14:12–14).

Unfortunately in our modern day, in practice if not in precept, prayer is pitted against work as its foe. Oswald Chambers says it well, "Prayer does not fit us for the greater works; prayer *is* the greater work."

The disciples, after seeing Jesus perform the miracle of feeding the thousands, asked a very significant question, "What shall we do that we might work the works of God?'' (John 6:28). Jesus' simple answer was, ''This is the work of God, that ye believe on him whom he hath sent'' (v. 29). How eager the disciples were to do the work of the kind they had seen Jesus doing. And so it is with us. But much of the work we are doing has little of the ring of a work of God. It may be a work for God, but it surely is not the work *of* God. There is a vital difference. I am convinced that the work of God is simply God at work in us in unhindered capacity and that all else is simply man's work for God which will come to naught. Now the significant thing about this is that prayer is the means by which this is implemented. Prayer is work, and without prayer there is no work.

E. M. Bounds says, ''Prayer is not the foe to work; it does not paralyze activity. It works mightily; prayer itself is the greatest work.''

We have in John 14:12–14, five great considerations of prayer as work.

First, there is the *declaration of the greater works*.

It is both impressive and relevant that as Jesus prepared his disciples for his own absence from them he informs them that the works of God will not cease with his leaving. There is only one qualification—''He that believes on me.''

Second, there is the *dimension of the greater works*.

He said that we would do the *same* works as he and that we would do those *surpassing* his works. He further adds that we are to ask anything in his name and we can expect to receive it.

Third, there is the *designation of the greater works*.

''And whatsoever you shall ask in my name.'' We are literally taking his place in prayer, standing in his stead as he stands in ours. The Amplified Version of the Bible uses the words ''presenting all that he is'' in each place where praying in the name of Jesus is mentioned. This is the designation by which we are to pray. That name represents all that he is, all that he has done, and all that he desires! We shall deal more fully with this later.

Fourth, there is the *dynamic of the greater works*.

Twice in this brief passage Jesus says, ''I will do it!'' That is the dynamic of our work—his doing! Prayer is releasing him in us to do that greater work.

Fifth, there is the *design of the greater work*.

"That the Father may be glorified in the Son." There is no doubt about the final design behind it all. The glory of God is the chief end of man and the final design of the universe. The location of all of this is "in the Son."

Thus we see that prayer is *work*. Man prays and worships God. Man prays and works toward kingdom consummation. There is a sense that as man prays he looks at God in worship and from worship serves the Lord in prayerful work toward others. Jesus revealed the secret of his works in John 5:17–19, "But Jesus answered them, My Father worketh hitherto, and I work. . . . Verily, verily, I say unto you, The Son can do nothing of himself, but what he seeth the Father do: for what things soever he doeth, these also doeth the Son likewise."

Now I want you to take time to grasp this. Do not rush over it! Jesus simply did what he saw the Father doing. That was the full nature of his work. Later in the same chapter he said, "I can of mine own self do nothing: as I hear, I judge: and my judgment is just; because I seek not mine own will, but the will of the Father which hath sent me" (v. 30). He not only *did* what he *saw*, but he *said* only what he *heard*. Now, that is a simple relationship. And he expects nothing more and nothing less of us. He did nothing he had not seen and said nothing he had not heard. He saw what God was up to and got in on it. He heard what God was saying and repeated it. And thus he did the works of God!

Now the question which will normally linger in your mind is this, "How did he know what God was doing, and how did he hear what God was saying?" That is a good question and it has a thrilling answer. Jesus communicated with the Father in constant prayer. He was first and foremost a person of prayer. The disciples recognized this when they asked him to teach to pray. We ask a person whom we recognize as an expert to teach us to do something. It is *with* our praying that God works. It is *while* we pray that God works. It is *because* we pray that God works. All that God does, he does through the agency of prayer. Through the means of prayer we find out where and what God is working and join him. Prayer was the main work of Christ while he was on earth. It is the main work of Christ now. "He ever liveth to make intercession for [us]" (Heb. 7:25). It is the main work of the Holy Spirit in us to intercede according to the intercessions that are being made for us in heaven. When we pray, we are simply cooperating with deity. We are always saying, "Let us pray and get to the work." When we pray, we are "to the work," the main work of the ministry. When we recognize that and further recognize that until we learn to pray we shall do no work which is God's work, we will be determined to pray! Find the secret of working *with* God in prayer.

Prayer as Warfare

Prayer is not only worship and work, it is also warfare. It is this missing facet in most praying that makes it empty ritual at worst and pious platitudes at best.

We shall see now why the devil fights prayer so determinedly and devotedly. We are informed of our awful engagement by Paul in Ephesians 6:10–12. "Finally, my brethren, be strong in the Lord, and in the power of his might. Put on the whole armour of God, that ye may be able to stand against the wiles of the devil. For we wrestle not against flesh and blood, but against principalities, against powers, against the rulers of the darkness of this world, against spiritual wickedness in high places." He then in detail describes and defines what the whole armor consists of. But at this point most of us have missed the issue. Where is the battle? It is one thing to be dressed for war; it is another thing to know where the battle is! I am not a military man but I do know that it is impossible to win a war if one does not know where the battle is being fought! We get more than a strong hint as to its location if we read on to verses 18–19. Verse 18 begins with the word *praying*.

Hear what S. D. Gordon said: "The greatest agency put into man's hands is prayer. And to define prayer one must use the language of war. Peace language is not equal to the situation. The earth is in a state of war and is being hotly beseiged. Thus one must use war talk to grasp the fact with which prayer is concerned. Prayer from God's side is communication between himself and his allies in the enemy country. True prayer moves in a circle. It begins with the heart of God and sweeps down into the human heart on earth, so intersecting the circle of the earth, which is the battlefield of prayer, and then goes back again to its starting point, having accomplished its purpose on the downward swing." [3] When we pray, we give God a footing in the battlefield! Hallelujah!

Every prayer *positively Godward* is *negatively Satanward*. It blesses God and bothers Satan. And that is to put it mildly. Prayer gets to the devil like nothing else we do. He has no defense system against prayer, for prayer throws the battle to the Lord, an engagement the devil has no stomach for. It is not Christian work that gets to the devil, it is prayer.

It is only in the place of prayer that we engage the devil. But before you panic at this fact, please be reminded that as you face the engagement it is with a victory already won for you on Calvary. You are in a very real sense simply updating a victory already won. You are standing in the incontestable authority of the crucified, risen, and ascended Lord and storming the battle lines of the enemy. If there is no prayer, there is no warfare. The only hope that the devil has is to stop the praying. When the praying stops, the warfare stops and the devil acts unhindered to seek to thwart the kingdom enterprises!

I have been so moved and blessed by a recent reading of Paul E. Billheimer's book on prayer, *Destined for the Throne*, that I must share some classic statements with you.

"The prayer closet is the *arena* which produces the overcomer. The world is a laboratory in which those destined for the throne are learning in actual practice how to overcome Satan and his hierarchy. This means that redeemed humanity outranks all other orders of created beings in the universe."

"The church, through her resurrection and ascension with Christ, is already legally on the throne. Through his use of her weapons of prayer and faith she holds in this present throbbing moment the balance of power in world affairs. In spite of all her lamentable weaknesses, appalling failures, and indefensible shortcomings, the church is the mightest force for civilization and enlightened social consciousness in the world today." The only force that is contesting Satan's total rule in human affairs is the church of the living God.

"She is, therefore, even now by virtue of the weapons of prayer and faith, engaged in 'on-the-job' training for her place as co-sovereign with Christ over the entire universe following Satan's final destruction."

"In order to enable the church to overcome Satan, God entered the stream of human history in the Incarnation. As unfallen man, He overcame and destroyed Satan both legally and dynamically. All that Christ did in redemption he did for the church. He is head over all things *to the church* (Eph. 1:22). His victory over Satan is accredited to the church. [Now get the next statement!] Although Christ's triumph over Satan is full and complete, God permits him to carry on guerrilla warfare. God could put Satan completely away, but he has chosen to use him to give the church on-the-job training in overcoming.'' [4] Praise the Lord!

So prayer is worship and looks toward God. Without prayer there is no worship.

Prayer is work and looks toward man as we work in man's behalf through prayer. Without prayer there is no vital work for God in behalf of man. It will amount to nothing!

Prayer is warfare against the devil! Without prayer there is no warfare and thus no victory. Prayer does not win the victory. It is the means by which an already-won victory is imposed over Satan here, now, and legally!

What is prayer? It is *worship*, *work*, and *warfare*—all three! If the church really believed the contents of this chapter and adjusted its priorities accordingly, I believe that we could see the greatest revival in the history of the church.

Friend, I must confess to you that at this moment I am fairly well overwhelmed with what my eyes have seen the last little while. I am at this writing in my favorite place with God—in my study in the woods. I am a simple country-bred preacher of average (or less) intelligence. I possess little or none of what the world calls charisma. I would have trouble getting a job if I wasn't preaching. This is not *humility*. It is *reality!* But at this moment I am thinking that from this spot I can touch three worlds and the beings in those worlds without leaving this spot. I can pray and touch heaven, God, his throne, and have influence among the angels through prayer. I can pray and touch the earth, its circumstances, its occupants, and its enterprises. I can pray and touch Satan, imposing a victory over him that is vested in the name of Jesus! In fact, if you will excuse me for a while, I believe I will pray! I suggest you mark your place, lay the book down, and join me! Shall we pray?

Lord, I thank you for the gift of prayer as a means of worshiping you. I praise you that through prayer I can get to know you. I bless

you that my first response to whitened harvest fields is to pray for
laborers to be thrust into the harvest. I give you thanks that the devil
is a defeated foe, that I have in the name of Jesus, legal victory over
Satan now! I exercise that authority now in Jesus' name. Teach me to
pray! In Jesus' name. Amen!

1. *Ibid.*, p. 25.
2. Armin R. Gesswein, *Seven Wonders of Prayer* (Grand Rapids: Zonder-van, 1957), p. 11.
3. S. D. Gordon, *Quiet Talks on Prayer* (New York: Pyramid Publications, 1967), p. 27.
4. Paul E. Billheimer, *Destined for the Throne* (Fort Washington, Pa.: Christian Literature Crusade, 1975), pp. 15–17.

6

The Cycle of Prayer

*True prayer moves in a circle. It begins in the heart of God,
sweeps down into the human heart upon the earth, so intersecting the circle of the earth, which is the battlefield of prayer, and
then it goes back again to its starting point, having accomplished its purpose on the downward swing (S. D. Gordon).* [1]

(The line drawings and the material set off in quotation marks in this
chapter are taken from *The Cycle of Prayer* by Ralph A. Herring,
published by Broadman Press in 1966. In 1973 the copyright was
reassigned to Mrs. Ralph A. Herring. © Copyright 1973 ● Mrs. Ralph
A. Herring. All rights reserved. Used by permission. Tyndale House
has issued *The Cycle of Prayer* as a Tyndale Treasure.)

A Cycle or Line?

How we look at prayer will determine how we pray. We shall not
rise in our practice of prayer above our perspective of prayer. It will
greatly help to get a biblical perspective on prayer. The biblical
perspective is God's perspective and that is the one that counts. What
you and I feel about prayer must be constructed on what God has said
about prayer.

There are at least two ways to look at the profile of prayer. We can
conceive it as a *line of communication* or as a *cycle*. Let us first
examine the idea of the line of communication. To visualize this you
would simply draw a line from man to God.

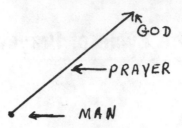

Now, while this idea has some transcendent truths, it does injustice to true prayer. Man can speak with God. God is listening and hears him when he prays. But there are some key problems in such a view of prayer. First, while the *invitation* is issued from God to pray, the *initiative* is left to man. The great problem with this idea is that it takes the initiative away from God. Second, it leaves man to his own wisdom as to how and what to pray.

It would be far better to consider prayer as a cycle. I believe that you will find a view of prayer here that will release the power of prevailing prayer as God involves us in this great adventure. God works in cycles. That he does is apparent even to the casual observer. The planet upon which we live is a circular sphere. The sun, likewise, is a sphere and around it in a vast ellipse our earth runs its course year by year. Because of the earth's angles of inclination, we have the seasons which run the cycle of spring, summer, fall, and winter. Every student of biology is acquainted with the "life cycle." Scientists use this phrase to describe the whole course of life without which no single state of its development could be understood. Even history moves in cycles. Art and music are familiar with the cycle.

Of special interest to our inquiry are the prepositions used in the declaration in Romans 11:36, "For of him, and through him, and to him are all things." *Of . . . through . . . to . . .* these words describe a circle, a cycle.

"The question naturally arises as to the relation of prayer to God's redemptive activity. Why are we about to consider the cycle of prayer rather than the cycle of some other experience of grace? The answer lies in the inclusive nature of prayer itself. It is God's triumph of spiritual engineering, employing all his gifts and providing unlimited access to all the resources of his being. Prayer is a summit meeting in the very throne room of the universe. There is no higher level. As all lines within the pyramid converge at its summit, so all the privileges of grace converge in prayer to God. . . . .

"Prayer epitomizes the divine-human encounter." To understand prayer is to have insight into this encounter.

"In discussing the cycle of prayer we are about to describe a circle. Arc will be added to arc to make the round complete. The point, however, is not in the roundness but in the circuit of divine energy represented by it. The circle is a symbol of perfection and that could throw us off. One must remember that life is not perfection. The saving energy which God has caused to flow from himself completes its cycle in spite of life's irregularities. The circuit is more like that of electricity than that of a geometric figure. In electricity it matters not how devious the course of the conduit. Power flows without interruption so long as there are two wires to complete the circuit. Energized prayer is like that."

The Level of Human Life

It is good to begin the search for truth right where we are. Thus we shall begin with the level of human life and go from there

THE LEVEL

OF HUMAN EXPERIENCE

FLOW OF TIME ⟶

"Human experience is depicted by the irregular line drawn from left to right. The 'ups and downs' are there to keep us mindful of the unevenness of life." Here, then, we make our beginning, here on the human level where all of us have something in common.

"Where shall we find the place along this line to mark the center of the circle?"

Let us ask another question to get the answer to this one. "What is the greatest thing that has happened on the level of human existence? John tells us. . . . 'The Word became flesh and dwelt among us' " (John 1:14, ASV). . . . Many great things can be said about the level of human experience, but the greatest is that the Son of God trod that path.

"Confirmation of the importance of the Jesus event in history came in due time and almost unconsciously. It did not happen by prearrangement or decree. Historians drifted into it and began dating events before Christ and after Christ. What else was there for them to do? They could find no experience on the human level of comparable significance. To Christians all other events must be secondary. Their relevance is derived from the incarnation of the Son of God. That fact is the criterion of history. The meaning of life is found in it.

THE HUMAN LEVEL   JESUS

~~~~~~~~~~~~~~~~~~~~~~~~~X~~~~~~~~~~~~~~~~~~

THE INCARNATION

John 1:14

"The incarnation of Christ, then, marks the point we seek. The circumference of our cycle of prayer is Christ-centered.

"We designate this center, aware that there is a timelessness about Christ's incarnation. His entrance into the human life-stream was from the very nature of the case an event which transcends all temporal limits. Being eternal, he is eternally current. For each of us he becomes continuingly the center of our predicament whatever may be our plight.

"Having found the center of the circle, the point of the circumference with which to begin becomes quite obvious. All prayer is directed to God. . . . Directly above the center, therefore, at the zenith of the cycle to be described, we shall place a mark under the phrase 'God Enthroned.' The Scripture reference, Hebrews 4:16, is appropriate and throws clear light upon the approach we are taking in this study. 'Let us therefore draw near with boldness unto the throne of grace, that we may receive mercy, and may find grace to help us in time of need' (ASV).

"Note that it is a *throne* to which we are encouraged to come, and that it is a throne of *grace*. Prayer would hold little meaning apart from the two great truths expressed here in a beautiful combination. That fact that we approach a throne of grace assures us, sinners as we are, of free access. We are invited to come with boldness through the ministry of a faithful high priest, 'one that hath been in all points tempted as we are, yet without sin' (Heb. 4:15, ASV). That it is a throne assures us, helpless as we are, that something can be done, and will be done in answer to our cry of distress."

Only a sovereign God can answer prayer. But there are many to whom his sovereignty is not very real. Their concept of God is more

GOD ENTHRONED
Heb. 4:16
X

THE HUMAN LEVEL   JESUS

that of a supreme power than of a supreme person. They see him so involved by the laws which he has established in his universe that he is not free to answer prayer. According to this point of view, miracles of deliverance and other supernatural inventions in behalf of his distressed people are ruled out because of the fixed nature of law. As a consequence, prayer becomes a vague longing, hardly more than wishful thinking. The logic of the position is inescapable: If God can do nothing, why bother to pray?

"But such a [concept] of God is not that of the Scriptures. The Bible reveals him as a person, sovereign and holy. He works his good pleasure in a manner consistent both with himself and with the law, which, having established, he nevertheless transcends. The prophet Isaiah was an exponent of this great truth. His constant theme was the sovereignty of God, 'the high and lofty that inhabiteth eternity, whose name is Holy' (Isa. 57:15). This emphasis grew out of his experience. He says, 'I saw the Lord . . . high and lifted up' (Isa. 6:1)."

"Only a sovereign God can inspire prayer and only a sovereign God can answer it. A man's concept of God, therefore, determines the depth of his prayer life. Real prayer begins and ends with God enthroned!

"But it takes more even than the concept of a sovereign . . . God to provide man with a sufficient incentive to [pray]. Left to his own resources, he is impotent. 'There is none that seeketh after God' (Rom. 3:11). This Scripture verse is confirmed by sad experience.

But there is another side to the picture. God has not left man to his own resources. His Spirit 'helpeth our infirmity' (Rom. 8:26, ASV) and supplies the energy needed to put prayer in orbit.

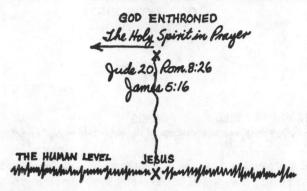

"We shall indicate this activity of God's Holy Spirit by an arrow, an appropriate symbol of movement and direction."

We shall use here another Scripture which is vital.

" 'The effectual fervent prayer of a righteous man availeth much' (Jas. 5:16)." The wide variety of translations invest this sentence with peculiar significance. It is well worth a study from this viewpoint alone. Dr. Herring's translation of this verse is, " 'Of mighty effect is the prayer of a righteous (man), energized as it is and (therefore) energizing.' " In other words the circuit of prayer is live; the line is *hot;* the voltage is high. From the beginning to the end the flow of effectual prayer throbs with God's energy. Like a true executive, the Holy Spirit is the great energizer and enabler through the prayer cycle."

The Divine Initiative

"The first arc in the circuit of prayer features the initiation of the divine impulse.

"We are naming it 'the divine initiative,' a term which theologians employ to describe the fact that God takes the first step in salvation. The opening verse of the Bible is the classic statement of this doctrine, 'In the beginning, God.' " He has made the claim to be the first and the last, the beginning and the end—" 'Alpha and the Omega' " (Rev. 1:8, ASV).

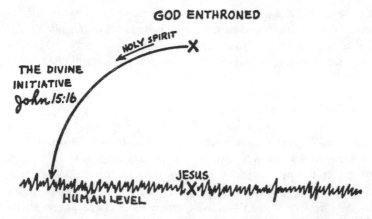

"Never once from the first verse to its closing benediction does the Bible reveal God as shrinking from or evading the responsibility of being *first*."

"The divine initiative in the realm of prayer is strikingly stated in John 15:16. Here emphasis falls upon God's choice or 'election,' another term by which theologians describe this same doctrine." Again Dr. Herring offers a helpful rendition, "It was not *you* (who) chose *me* (as you might think), but I (who in my sovereign grace) chose *you*, and I placed you (in such circumstances) that you might go (*i.e.*, be at ease, feeling free to go and come) and bear fruit and that your fruit might abide (all with the further purpose) that *whatever* you ask the Father in my name *he will give it you*."

"In this passage we see that prayer forms both climax and conclusion to one of the strongest statements on election to be found in the Bible. God's sovereign choice, therefore, does not impair or paralyze man's initiative. Rather it honors that initiative as the quality in man which most strikingly marks him as being created in God's likeness. Prayer is made up of interplay between the divine will and the human, and for that reason it faithfully shows how man's will becomes freed and fulfilled in God's. Man gains the mastery for which he was originally created through the exercise of prayer, and the highest inspiration for him to gain this mastery is God himself."

Now, it should be clear what is being said here, namely that whatever there is in prayer that he can honor was put there by him in the first place. Many a person makes the mistake of coming to God as if to say, "Here, Lord, is something I thought up all by myself (or some of us together worked it out and included it in our plans). All that is needed now is your blessing. Grant it we pray." Many a committee meeting or business session in the council halls of Zion has followed this pattern. Men work out their plans and in a closing prayer ask God's blessings upon them, forgetting that God waits to bless that which he has himself begun.

There is another significant implication brought out by the divine initiative. "Prayer means more to God than it means to us. He is more desirous to answer than we are to ask. . . . If God initiates prayer, it follows logically that he does so for the satisfaction of desires that burn within his own nature. His grand purposes await fulfilment in man's active participation in the adventure of faith." . . .

The Point of Need

"In some ways the most exciting port of call in our adventure along the circumference of this cycle is that which we shall indicate on our [diagram] as the point of need. Here the divine initiative engages man upon the human level.

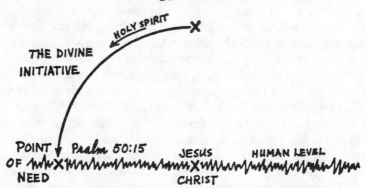

"In Matthew 6:8 Jesus indicates that petition grows out of the awareness of need. 'Your Father knoweth what things ye have need of, before ye ask him.' " The psalmist records God as saying, " 'Call upon me in the day of trouble; and I will deliver thee, and thou shalt glorify me.' "

"Sooner or later trouble overtakes us all." We have been warned in the Scripture of this fact. We should not be surprised or distressed when the Scripture proves again to be true. Trouble renders a significant service in the providence of God—they bring us to him in prayer. They articulate the inadequacy which previously we had only vaguely felt." It is the opinion of Dr. Herring [and mine] that "the divine initiative, or God's call, is more frequently communicated to man in his awareness of need than through any other medium."

"Jesus . . . chooses the point of need as his most likely meeting place with man." It is vital "that we grasp the full significance of need in God's great purpose. He wants us to interpret our need in terms of its final resolution in our need of *him*. . . . Let us learn, . . . then, . . . to glory in adversity, knowing that God's power is made perfect in our weakness!"

Asking

The idea of continuity is essential to any circumference. The various parts merge one with another in a constantly flowing stream. "We have already seen how adversity supplies the friction for the match which lights the fuse of desire. . . .

"Notice that the path leads downward as the intensity of the prayer burden brings the suppliant to humble himself [under] the mighty hand of God.

"Desire has a very real part in the making of prayer. Indeed, it might be described as the soul of prayer." Do not be afraid to present your desires to the Father. That is the starting place of answered prayer as far as the human is concerned. It is at this place that he joins the cycle of prayer, at the point of his desire which arose out of need! So he is simply encouraged to ask! Luke 11:9–10, "And I say unto you, Ask and it shall be given you; seek, and ye shall find; knock, and it shall be opened unto you."

"Because desire is so important, I counsel those who are interested in vitalizing their prayer life to make the most of it. Begin where you are rather than where you think you ought to be. Ask God for the things you want . . . Begin *there*. God does.

"God places such high value on our desire because our desire is the only vehicle upon which he can lay his own." The best way for God to get his desires is to plant them in us and have us pray for

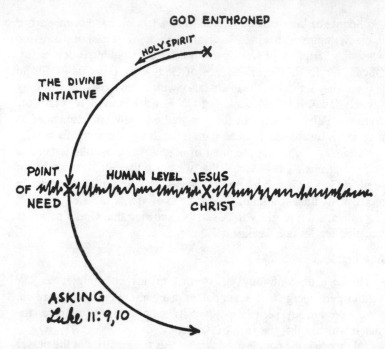

them! Our longings reveal our affinity for him. If our desires are childish, then a child can learn. If our stated desires are hypocritical, we really don't mean them, then God can do nothing.''

The Crisis

"We are now at the nadir of the circle, its 'inferior pole'—the place of crisis." God and man are poles apart. Paul learned to exult in the paradox of this position. "When I am weak, then am I strong" (2 Cor. 12:10, ASV). We depend greatly in this hour upon the Spirit's illumination. In this crisis we yield, but our yielding is to claim. We turn loose but our turning loose is to take. There is surrender here to superior providence. We turn from ourselves to him. The cross is stationed squarely between us and him. The grand lesson for this crisis is to leave the choice to him. Someone has said, "He always gives the best to those who leave the choice to him." The disposition of this hour is, "Thy will be done."

"No experience recorded in the Scriptures better illustrates what happens in this crisis than that of Jacob." It is the need that drives Jacob to the meeting place where his will is to be exchanged for God's. In fact, you can clearly trace the circle in Jacob's experience.

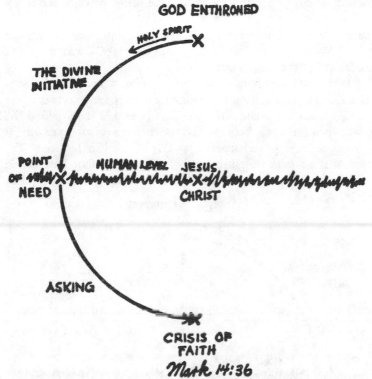

We see the *divine initiative* in selecting Jacob from the beginning as the one through whom God's redemptive plans will be carried out.

As rebellious as Jacob was, the Spirit of God was present ready to pray when Jacob turned to the Lord. His *point of need* came when Esau came for a showdown. The arc of Jacob's 'asking' came when he faced the prospects of the showdown. However, the showdown came with God, not Esau. God may arrange one set of circumstances in which we believe we are about to face someone else and behold, there he [God] is!

"And Jacob was left alone; and there wrestled a man with him until the breaking of the day" (Gen. 32:24, ASV). God would touch him and that touch would at once defeat him and yet be his victory, paralyze him and enable him. Then came the cry, the desperate cry of a desperate man. There is the crisis, when a man would get God's blessing at any price! That came with the facing of who God really was—the most difficult thing for any human being to admit. "My name is Jacob." That was more than just an identification of who he was. "My name is cheat, fraud, trickster, fake" was the frank confession of the broken man.

"When man sees himself as God sees him, when from the heart man accepts the judgment that God pronounces and executes at the cross, when openly and willingly man takes his stand before the world upon the word that God gives,—then *the crisis is passed.*"

And the redemptive nature of the crisis is clear only then. "Thy name shall no more be called Jacob, but Israel: for thou hast striven with God and [note the order] with men, and hast prevailed" (Gen. 32:28, ASV).

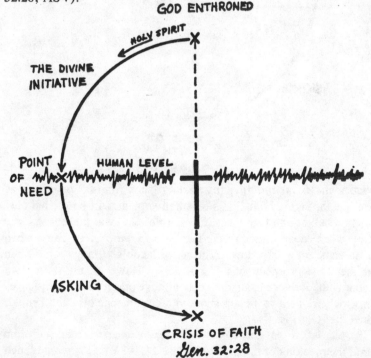

GOD ENTHRONED

HOLY SPIRIT

THE DIVINE
INITIATIVE

POINT
OF
NEED

HUMAN LEVEL

ASKING

CRISIS OF FAITH
Gen. 32:28

Claiming

"The next arc in our journey is probably the least understood in the cyclorama of prayer. We shall designate it by the word *claiming*, but there is much more to it than that. The way leads upward. This section marks the calm assurance with which the suppliant emerges from the crisis experience. An appropriate passage is 1 John 5:14–15 which begins, 'This is the boldness.'

"It may seem surprising to introduce the idea of boldness so closely after the humility learned in the crisis-experience just described. But boldness in prayer is quite in keeping with humility; it is in fact the ripe fruit of humility and is, therefore, of a special delight to God. The reason so many of our prayers are timid is not because of humility. . . . Why should we be timid if we are really asking in Jesus' name for that which the Father himself wants done?"

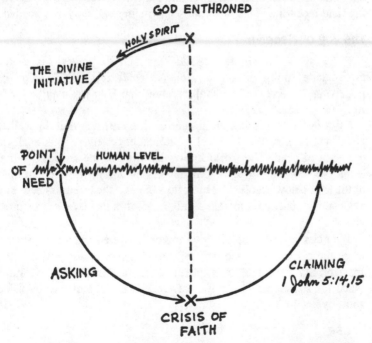

In 1 John 5:14–15 it is clear that our asking in God's will means God *hearing*, and his *hearing* means our *having*! "One then comes

out of the crisis" with the faith that he has met and heard from God and has prayed in God's will. He then possesses " 'the title deed of things hoped for.' That is precisely the idea in the word translated *substance* in Hebrews 11:1."

The curve of the arc is upward. That is the direction after the crisis. That has been the reason for the crisis, that we may be directed toward God. There is thus a peace which passeth understanding because it rests not on outer circumstances but the inner things we are certain of (*i.e.,* "hoped for") in Hebrews 11:1.

It is at this point that there is generally another crisis in waiting. There is sometimes a waiting period between asking and actually receiving. It is here that many a saint breaks down in his faith. He is not the "waiting kind," yet this is vital in the pilgrimage with the Father. Worry while waiting slanders every promise of God. This is apt to be the point of greatest satanic attack, between asking, claiming, and receiving. This is where "maintainence" prayer is needed.

The Joy of Receiving

"The next point in the cyclic approach to prayer" is at the three-quarter point on the circle. We shall call it "The Joy of Receiving." "Ask, and ye shall receive, that your joy may be made full" (John 16:24, ASV).

"But before exploring the nature of this joy, we shall do well to pause and look across the level of human experience, back again to the point of need. The world knows but little of the area above that level. Nor can it know the agonized seeking and the triumphant faith of the area below that level. But it lays to heart the point of need, and against that background takes full note of this place of manifest victory."

Who can describe the glorious joy of answered prayer, especially when the claim was made before, the faith-stand was firm, and the answer fully expected! It is sinful to be surprised when we have asked for something in the will of God. It is not sinful to be filled with joy!

Praise

"The cycle of prayer concludes fittingly in praise to God." The term "unto the praise of his glory" is the end of all things. We remember at the outset that "For of him, and through him, and to him are all things" (Rom. 11:36, ASV).

"If the preceding arc" of claiming "was rightly described as the least understood, . . . by the same token this final arc may be called the most neglected. Great is the pity, too, because we are at the stage of completion." Nothing else on the cycle substitutes for it. It is the divine followthrough for all petitions. As in athletics, the follow-through brings increased power and direction. There is a distinction between thanksgiving and praise. They are alike in many respects. They are the twin daughters of gratitude, though not identical. Thanksgiving may be the first expression of gratitude. Praise may come later. Thanksgiving may enumerate the blessings received. Praise adores the giver of the blessings.

"Genuine praise is witnessing at its best. It is the highest form of testimony." It completes the blessed cycle and lands us with God in the deepest expressions of divine-human love. It is here that we realized the *end* of all things is not in *things* but in *him*! We are to praise him for himself. What he gives in the way of tangibles can be

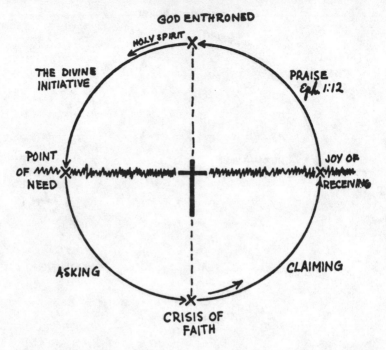

taken away. We praise him not for what he gives but what he is. That is victory!

"The wheel has come full circle. As we have traced our adventure in prayer along its circumference, familiar landmarks have come to view. New insights have yielded fresh encouragement. Some of us have discovered our place and progress in the prayer assignment now engrossing our deepest longings." Sometimes it is years between the spans of that circle. There is no limit to the depth and variety of experiences. "But whether in one cycle or many, our involvement turns by God's sovereign grace around Jesus Christ the Lord. He is center and circumference. Thus, we come again and with new meaning to the point at which we began.

" 'O the depth of the riches both of the wisdom and the knowledge of God! how unsearchable are his judgments, and his ways past finding out! For who hath known the mind of the Lord? or who hath been his counsellor? or who hath first given to him, and it shall be recompensed unto him again? For of him, and *through* him, and *unto* him, are all things. To him be the glory for ever. Amen' '' (Rom. 11:33–36, ASV).

---

1. Gordon, *op. cit.*, p. 27.

7

In the Name of Jesus

And whatsoever ye shall ask in my name, that will I do, that the Father may be glorified in the Son. If you shall ask any thing in my name, I will do it (John 14:13–14).

And in that day ye shall ask me nothing. Verily, verily, I say unto you, Whatsoever ye shall ask the Father in my name, he will give it you. Hitherto have ye asked nothing in my name: ask, and ye shall receive, that your joy may be full (John 16:23–24).

I have approached this chapter with much care and some fear. The truths involved in the material designated by the title could change your life! For that reason, I write with care. Only God can reveal the implications of these truths to your heart. Thus, the presence of some fear that either the representation will be inadequate or your ability to receive impaired. Would you pause now to pray, as I have in the writing for the Holy Spirit to grant you this desire, "That you might be filled with the knowledge of his will in all wisdom and spiritual understanding" (Col. 1:9).

A Repeated Consideration

Over and over again in the Scriptures we read, "In my name," "In Jesus' name," or "In his name." The use and power of the name of Jesus did not begin with the dispensation of the Spirit. While Jesus was a contemporary in the flesh, walking among men, his name was mighty. In Luke 9:1 we read, "Then he called his twelve disciples together, and gave them power and authority over all devils, and to cure diseases." He then sent them away. Upon their return they were filled with joy because, "Even the devils are subject unto us *through thy name*" (Luke 10:17).

Prior to that experience Jesus had given hint of the implications of his name. Having set a child by him, he said, "Whosoever shall receive this child *in my name* receiveth me: and whosoever shall receive me receiveth him that sent me" (Luke 9:48).

We are informed that folks can gather together in that name. "For where two or three are gathered together in my name, there am I in the midst of them" (Matt. 18:20).

We are commanded to baptize in the name of the Father, Son, and Holy Spirit (Matt. 28:19).

In that passage that is under question in the latter part of Mark, we read, "In my name shall they cast out devils; and they shall speak with new tongues; they shall take up serpents; and if they drink any deadly thing, it shall not hurt them; they shall lay hands on the sick, and they shall recover" (Mark 16:17–18). Parenthetically, I might say that, though this passage does not appear in some manuscripts, there is nothing in it that contradicts what we believe. It is a mistake, however, to use this passage to justify all that is going on in these days as genuine. Devils were cast out in that name. They spoke with new tongues. Paul was miraculously spared harm when a deadly snake attached itself to his hand. The sick were healed and other harm miraculously averted. The significant thing here is that all this was done in Jesus' name.

We are to give thanks to God in that name. "Giving thanks always for all things unto God and the Father in the name of our Lord Jesus Christ."

Among the first apostolic miracles after Pentecost was the raising of the lame man at the gate of the Temple. To that man Peter said, "Silver and gold have I none; but such as I have give I thee: In the name of Jesus Christ of Nazareth rise up and walk" (Acts 3:6). In making later explanation of this miracle Peter said, "And his name through faith in his name hath made this man strong, whom ye see and know" (Acts 3:16). And still later he explained, "Be it known unto you all, and to all the people of Israel, that by the name of Jesus Christ of Nazareth, whom ye crucified, whom God raised from the dead, even by him doth this man stand here before you whole" (Acts

4:10).

Peter, in the same discourse, declared, "There is none other *name* under heaven given among men, whereby we must be saved" (v. 12).

A council was called as a result of that miraculous healing and it was decided by the council that the disciples should be straightly threatened, "That they [should] speak henceforth to no man in this name. And they called them, and commanded them not to speak at all nor teach in the name of Jesus (vv. 17–18).

After Saul's conversion on the Damascus road and his subsequent rejection by the other disciples at Jerusalem because of fear, Barnabas took him and "declared unto them how he (Saul) had seen the Lord in the way, and that he had spoken to him, and how he preached boldly at Damascus *in the name of Jesus.*

We are further told, "Whosoever shall call upon the name of the Lord shall be saved" (Rom. 10:13).

We have been "justified in the name of the Lord Jesus, and by the Spirit of Our God" (1 Cor. 6:11).

Though there are many other references to his name, it will suffice to summarize by Paul's exhortation in Colossians 3:17, "And whatsoever ye do in word or deed, do all in the name of the Lord Jesus, giving thanks to God and the Father by him."

No wonder we are moved to sing the song made famous by Bill Gaither, "There's just something about that name!"

Frederick Whitfield wrote in 1855:

> There is a name I love to hear,
> I love to sing its worth;
> It sounds as music in mine ear,
> The sweetest name on earth.
> Oh, how I love Jesus,
> Oh, how I love Jesus,
> Oh, how I love Jesus,
> Because he first loved me.

While this is true, I greatly fear that few folks indeed have much of a clue of what it means to operate in the name of Jesus.

While I want you to see the far-reaching implication of the name of Jesus, our consideration here will be the privilege of *praying in his name.* He has invited, urged, and commanded us to pray in his name.

What does it mean to be able to pray in the name of Jesus? In the next pages I trust that the Lord will apply to your heart some vital truths that have greatly blessed me.

A Word of Warning

Whatever it means to pray in the name of Jesus, I am certain that it involves more than words. This is no magic formula tacked onto an assembly of words which, despite the motive, give it credibility with the Father. I am convinced that many have been the times when we have dutifully said, "In Jesus' name," in ending our prayer without really praying in his name. For to pray in his name is more than a *declaration*, it is a *disposition*. We are *in Christ* as a result of the mighty regenerating work of the Holy Spirit. As we act under the full implications of being in Christ and having him *in us* we will be less apt to seek our way and more apt to seek his. A basic understanding of what it means to pray in Jesus' name will not only serve to prevent wrongful praying but also will open the door into a level of prayer heretofore unknown.

Three Illustrations

It must be understood that any illustration of a great truth cannot fully convey the vast expanse of that truth's meaning. It does, however, generally give us a point of reference in helping us to begin to understand that truth.

Let me first point out the *rod of Moses* in Exodus 4. You will remember that Moses had begun his ministry forty years before, only to miserably fail in his own energy. God has reissued the call and made clear that he (God) would provide the power by which the people of God would be delivered from Egyptian bondage. After that discourse in Exodus 3, Moses said, "But, behold, they will not believe me nor hearken unto my voice: for they will say, The Lord hath not appeared unto thee" (Ex. 4:1). What followed was a unique experience with Moses' rod. He was ordered by the Lord to throw it down, whereupon it immediately became a snake. Moses did the only sensible thing to do, he fled! But the Lord called him back, now ordering him to pick it up again—this time by the tail! As Moses obeyed, the serpent became a rod again in Moses' hand! That rod, in the hand of Moses, now was the credential of authority, calling what

God was into the situation. The problem before was that Moses did all that Moses could do. That simply was not enough. Now, armed with the relationship of God in which God would provide both *direction* and *dynamics*, the task would be done. With that rod (and all that it implied) Moses defeated the magicians of Egypt, brought the plagues upon the land, opened the Red Sea for that miraculous crossing, brought water out of the rock, and defeated Amalek in the Valley of Rephidim! I ask you, was it the rod that did all that? No, the rod was a catalyst, a credential, which, provided by God, brought God into the affair with all his power. Before that experience of total submission to God on Moses' part that rod could do nothing more than a man could do. But now, with God's hand on his life, Moses could be used to do what God wanted to do! Now, this is what I want you to see: All that the rod was in the hand of Moses, the name of Jesus is to us. It brings all that God is in Christ into the situation prayed for as well as the one who prays. It is the only credential needed to turn the tide in the battle, to open a miraculous path through the problem, or to bring provision in times of despairing want!

Second, I point out the simple illustration of *marriage*. In recent centuries it has become the custom in many lands that the bride bear the name of the husband. In the marriage ceremony she is legally placed *into* the name of her husband. Let us suppose that a bride is very poor in every way. She has no money in the bank, no real estate, no borrowing power, no earning power, no record of any worth at all. But the moment she becomes "Mrs." she moves out of the realm of her past and into all that the name of her husband means. Let us suppose that he is very rich in every way. He has hundreds of thousands of dollars in the bank, sprawling real-estate interests, millions of dollars in potential credit open to him, tremendous earning capacity, and a phenomenal record of worth in general. The "Mrs.," from the moment that she became his wife, identifies with all of that. She no longer acts in her name but in his! She can spend money from his bank, live on his real estate, operate on his borrowing power, enjoy his earnings, and live in the splendor of all that he is worth! Do you see? The church, "betrothed to become Mrs. Jesus," if you please, has been authorized to operate *in the name of Jesus!* Hallelujah!

Now the third illustration to which I refer is one from the legal field—*the power of attorney*. As you know this is a legal arrangement whereby one person may represent another in his absence in a certain matter or matters. It is often necessary for me, in pursuit of this ministry, to travel abroad. I have an arrangement by which my wife is given authorization to act in my absence in matters which would otherwise demand my presence. Now and again it is necessary for *both* of us to be out of the country. In this case, someone else is designated to have the power of attorney in certain matters. They may act in behalf of our family interests and in our place. There is *specific* power of attorney which designates the matter or matters in which a person may act to another's behalf. There is also *general* power of attorney which authorizes one to act in *all* matters pertaining to another who is absent. Jesus has given every believer unlimited and general power of attorney in all matters and with this the right to use his name in every situation! I would be moved to exclaim, "The sky is the limit!" but that would be erroneous, not even the sky is the limit!

So with these three illustrations in mind let us view the considerations at hand which are involved in praying in the name of Jesus!

I present several words for your consideration which will shed light on this tremendous area of truth.

The first is *renunciation*. When we respond to the command to pray in Jesus' name, we are admitting the bankruptcy of our own name. We are renouncing our own worth and merit at the throne of grace. We are admitting that in our flesh dwells no good thing, that we have no worth whereby his grace to claim. If I were to attempt to pray in my name, I would find that my prayer would have no more worth or result than the worth of the name in which it was prayed. Therefore, gladly I pray, disclaiming any credit and walking out of my name into his name. Like the bride coming from abject poverty to marry the wealthy husband, we may sing, "Out of my want and into thy wealth . . . Jesus, I come to Thee."

The next word is *identification*. To pray in Jesus' name is to pray under an assumed name. But, praise the Lord, the assumption is perfectly legal and duly encouraged! We are to pray in identity with the person of Jesus. All that Jesus did in his earthly life was *for us*. All that he sent the Holy Spirit to do after his ascension was *for us*.

All that he now does at his position at God's right hand is *for us*. All
that he is he is *for us*. I can thus *identify* with all that he did as if I had
done it myself. *It is as much mine as if I had, in my own merit,
accomplished it!* Think about it! He died for you. When you by faith
identified with that death, it was savingly effective for you. You
entered into the penalty for all your sins in him. Further, you, being
placed into him by the Holy Spirit, may identify with him in resurrection. If he died, then you died also. Reckoning your death *with* him
just as you reckoned his death *for* you, there comes the reality of a
new life. Paul was doing precisely this when he said, "I am crucified
with Christ." But this is not all. We are identified with him in victory
over the devil. In his name we have the same authority over the
powers of darkness he has! We are identified with him in authority
and power. We shall be identified with him at his coming. We shall
be identified with him in the ages to come. That identification is *legal*
and *total*. We stand in a position of total identification. "As he is, so
are we in this world" (1 John 4:17).

The next word is *possession*. Jesus has literally given us his name!
It is ours by legal possession. What does that mean? What is in a
name? All that the name means is all that the person means. A person
is identified by his name. All that Jesus was, his name is and *to have
his name is to have himself. He has given us himself*, represented by
his name. "And hath put all things under his feet, and gave him to be
head over all things *to the church*, which is his body, the fulness of
him that filleth all in all" (Eph. 1:22–23). Did you notice the words,
"and gave him . . . to the church"? I then have the liberty to say in
every situation, "For this I have Jesus." *He* is in his name. When I
use that name, I am confessing that he is mine and that I am his!

Our next word is *submission*. "But I thought that to pray in the
name of Jesus was to pray with authority!" you may exclaim. Yes,
but as Jesus' authority rested with his submission to the Father, so
our authority rests with our submission to him. To pray in his name is
to ask by his authority; and to ask by his authority is to ask in
accordance with his will as revealed in his Word. Thus submission
to the will of God is a vital matter in praying in Jesus' name. As I
pray in Jesus' name, I am identifying with all his desires and
determinations for mankind. I am admitting that all of what I ask for
is for Jesus' sake. To ask in his name is to ask according to his nature,

and his nature is one of submission!

Another vital word is *representation*. As I come to the Father in Jesus' name, I am fulfilling my privilege of representing him and his interests here on earth. Having the power of attorney means that I can act in his name, in his behalf, in accord with his best interests in every matter pertaining to him. Mystery of mysteries that with all the praying Jesus is doing, he yet desires that I represent him in prayer as if I must provide that which is lacking. I must pray for the lost, representing Jesus. I must resist the devil as a representative of Jesus. As his representative, I must invite folks to the Father. And withal I must pray without ceasing in that name representing all that he is and all that he has done!

Finally, I suggest the word *expectation*. If I prayed in my name, I could only expect such results to accrue as fitted the worthiness of my name. But since I pray in Jesus' name, I may expect the answer in accord with the value of his name. So I can pray with great and excited *expectation*. I have come to the throne of grace at the invitation of and in the name of the Lord Jesus Christ and have every right to expect exactly what would be expected if Jesus, himself, was there! (And indeed he is in appearance at God's right hand and in essence, by his Spirit, in me!) So when we pray in the name of Jesus, we can know the practice of prayer *with expectation*.

Presenting All That He Is

In the Amplified Version of the Bible, each time that the words "the name of Jesus" occur there are added these words in parentheses, "Presenting all that he is." I like that. When I pray in his name, I am presenting to the Father all that is in that name, which is all that he is, as a reason for my accessibility to the throne as well as the reason to expect to be heard and answered. But to pray in his name is even more than presenting all that he is, it is *standing* in all that he is, *identified* totally with him. Thus, I am not only presenting *all that he is* but *all that I am in him*. As I pray from that vantage point, prayer is vital and prevailing! I, alone, am not worthy that God should listen to one of my prayers. But since I have been converted, I have not been alone and have no right to discuss myself as being alone. I have not been alone since I met him. We became *one* then! To discuss me is to discuss him! We go together! Praying in his name asserts that consciously we are together. The enemy has only to rob me of that conscious fact (that I am in him and he is in me) to defeat me. Losing consciousness of who he is in me and who I am in him will mean *practical* defeat in the midst of *positional* victory!

Conclusion

Now we know that God has given to Jesus a name which is above every name: and at that name will bow every knee with the admission from every tongue that Jesus Christ is Lord! (see Phil. 2:9–11).

In the meanwhile, we have been given that name by which to do all things. We are to pray in that name, that is, in all that he is, all that he has ever been, all that he has done, and all that he is now doing! I own all this as mine as I pray in his name.

Jesus has bequeathed us his name—the full power of attorney to act in his behalf. But the great thing about that is that we act in his behalf with himself in us while we are doing it! All that Jesus is he is in his name and he is all!

His standing in the court of the Father is my standing in the court of the Father! Those words, "In the name of Jesus," are not like a good-luck charm which sends the prayer on its way. Those words link my prayer with Christ himself. He is the high priest of our confession.

We are saved by calling upon the name of Jesus. We are baptized into the name of Jesus. We are to pray in the name of Jesus. We are in Christ, and have legal right to use that name. This glorifies the Father, magnifies the Son, and answers the need of humanity.

The unlimited use of the name implies the confidence that God still has in the church. That privilege has not been withdrawn.

We could spend our time trying to analyze, or theorize, or argue. But Jesus said, "Whatsoever ye shall ask the Father in my name, I will give it you," and we had best start acting like we believe he told the truth!

"Hitherto have ye asked nothing in my name: ask, and ye shall receive, that your joy may be full" (John 16:24).

8

Praying in the Spirit

It is the easiest thing in a hundred to fall from power to form, but it is the hardest thing of many to keep in the life, spirit and power of any one duty, especially prayer; that is such a work that a man without the help of the Spirit cannot so much as pray once, much less continue without, in a sweet praying frame, and in praying, so to pray as to have his prayers ascend unto the ears of the Lord of the Sabaoth (John Bunyan in PRAYER).

If anyone were to ask me what is the first truly great secret of a successful prayer life, I would say in answer, "Praying in the Holy Spirit!" (Lehman Strauss). [1]

[Praying] always with all prayer and supplication in the Spirit, and [watch] thereunto with all perseverance and supplication for all saints (Eph. 6:18).

But ye, beloved, [build] up yourselves on your most holy faith, praying in the Holy Ghost (Jude 20).

We have already become acquainted with the helplessness of unhelped prayer. Prayer was not provided to be carried on alone. In fact there can be no true prayer without the aid of the Holy Spirit. "[He] helpeth our infirmities" (Rom. 8:26). It will be helpful at this point to discuss briefly the subject of *praying in the Spirit*.

The only two contexts for this statement are quoted above in Ephesians 6:18 and Jude 20. And yet the nature of the subject is so vital that if we miss this secret, we shall miss prayer in total.

Though these are the only two mentions as such regarding praying in the Spirit, there are other matters mentioned involving "in the Spirit." Perhaps an understanding of the context of these will aid us in understanding better what it means to pray in the Spirit.

Jesus told the woman at the well, "God is a Spirit: and they that worship him must worship him in spirit and in truth" (John 4:24). Now in this case, Jesus seems to be talking about the *realm* of the spirit, rather than the person of the Holy Spirit. God is a Spirit and to do anything vital to the life of God, it must be done in the realm of the spirit with the Holy Spirit presiding.

Man was made in the beginning to reign in his spirit. Sin dethroned the life of the spirit and the soul and body reigned. It is the purpose and plan of God in redemption to re-enthrone the spirit by entering a man and filling him with his Holy Spirit. In that manner man's spirit, recreated by the work of the Holy Spirit, can reign spiritually.

Paul said, "Walk in the Spirit, and ye shall not fulfil the lust of the flesh" (Gal. 5:16). The context here doubtlessly suggests the realm of obedience to the Holy Spirit. To walk in the Spirit is to walk under his control, according to his nature, fulfilling his desires. The opposite of this is "walking in the flesh." This does not necessarily mean walking in immorality. The flesh refers to what a man is apart from the divine nature. To walk in the flesh is to walk in oneself, his own nature, his own desires, fulfilling the natural desires of the body and the soul.

Later on, Paul said, "If we live in the Spirit, let us also walk in the Spirit" (Gal. 5:25). Again, it is clear that the implication is the same, that is, walking in accord with the life-style of the Spirit of God. We were reminded earlier that "They that are Christ's have crucified the flesh with the affections and lusts" (Gal. 5:24). That is to be kept in mind (and kept current) as the Spirit would lead us to prayer. The prayer place is no place for the bearing of fleshly interests. When the flesh takes over, prayer leaves! There may be prayers said, but there is no vital praying apart from the Holy Spirit presiding to bring to bear in our praying the Father's own desires.

God is the source of all true prayer. Praying to God in the Spirit is praying to God under God's control.

An Ominous Alternative

As I have already implied, there is no true prayer without the direction and dynamics of the Holy Spirit. When a man calls upon God for saving efficacy, that was not the first call. The first call was from the Spirit of God in the heart of that man. And from that time all true prayer, as at the beginning, is a work of the Holy Spirit *through* the believer. And with the use of the term *through*, I want to straighten out a prevailing misconception. I hear many people praying to Jesus and I believe that it is only right to heap upon Jesus adulations and love. But to pray as to leave out the Father is to leave something out of prayer. Jesus expressly said, "And in that day, ye shall ask me nothing. Verily, verily, I say unto you, Whatsoever ye shall ask the Father in my name, he will give it you" (John 16:23). Now, the key words are "in that day." We found similar words in John 14:20, "At that day ye shall know that I am in my Father, and ye in me, and I in you." These are obvious references to a time in the future when a basic arrangement will be changed. I believe that Jesus was doubtlessly referring to Pentecost and the incoming of the Spirit into every believer. Thus, Jesus was saying, "The arrangement is different. You have been asking me for things and I have supplied them. Now, ask the Father, through the Spirit, in my name and it will be given you. In fact, what you ask in my name I will do it!" (see John 14:14).

There is only one alternative to praying in the Spirit and that is praying in the flesh, if that can be called praying at all.

Prerequisites for Praying in the Spirit

First, in order to be able to pray in the Spirit, *one must be born of the Spirit*. There is no command for the sinner to pray in the Spirit. He is to call upon the Lord for salvation. The promises of prayer are not for outsiders. They belong only to those who have been born again of the Spirit of God.

Second, to be able to pray in the Spirit *one must be filled with the Spirit*. When a person is born again, he is placed into Christ in a glorious Spirit-baptism which never again needs to be repeated. He is water-baptized to show forth that he has been Spirit-baptized. If Spirit-baptism has not taken place, water baptism is empty and meaningless. Also when a person is born again, he is, at least for the time being, filled with the Spirit. The Spirit has entered him. Jesus is his Lord. But if that believer is not taught the precepts of spiritual living and the arrangements God has provided for triumphant living, he will backslide. The tragedy is that he will, much of the time, find little help from fellow Christians! The sad fact is that he, in most surroundings, is forced to backslide in order to have fellowship with other believers! Because of this possibility, we are enjoined to "be continuously being filled with the Spirit" (see Eph. 5:18). Few have been the believers I have met who did not seriously backslide after their conversion and need the experience of being filled again with the Holy Spirit. It is a divine command to be filled with the Spirit. There can be no victorious, prevailing prayer (if any prayer at all) with divine commands unheeded in the life. *I repeat, it is impossible to pray in the Spirit without being filled with the Spirit.*

Of course, inherent in being filled with the Spirit on a continuing basis will be the process of walking in the Spirit and living in the Spirit (Gal. 5:25). The event of being filled with the Spirit as an experience is vital as the gateway to a life led of the Spirit, lived in the Spirit, and controlled by the Spirit. It is shocking to realize that before we are filled with the Spirit there is little real prayer, if any at all!

Abiding in Christ is another way of stating the prerequisite of praying in the Spirit. Of course, these matters cannot be divided because to be filled with the Spirit is to be controlled by the indwelling Christ. To be abiding in Christ is to be filled with the Spirit. One cannot abide in Christ without the work of the Spirit. But there is another vital matter, namely, *allowing his Word to abide in us.* Many a prayer life breaks down at this point and we shall discuss this more fully under the chapter on prayer and the Word. Jesus said, "If ye abide in me, and my words abide in you, ye shall ask what you will, and it shall be done unto you" (John 15:7). This dual abiding will prepare us to pray in the Spirit. In fact this dual abiding will guarantee that we will pray in the Spirit for such prayer is the inevitable outcome of such an abiding life just as fruit is the result of a healthy vine.

Another prerequisite is simply *time*. It takes time to pray God's way because it takes time to get to know God. The reason for prayer is getting to know God. For want of time, many a Christian's life is barren. It takes time to know God and one cannot love God in the truest sense without knowing him. Then as one comes to really know God and as a result has a heart filled with love for him, it will then take more time to fulfill that love in the experience of prayer. Prayer is loving God. It is not so much a *ritual* as it is a *relationship*. Hurry is the death of prayer. We inevitably desire to spend much time with that which we love the most!

Conclusion

Let us summarize what it means to pray in the Spirit.

First, it is to pray *with the Spirit's cooperation*. He *helps* our infirmities; that is he cooperates with us in the joint venture of prayer (Rom. 8:26).

Second, it is to pray *under the Spirit's control*. While prayer is a cooperative venture, it is a venture which is under control of the Senior Partner. Watchman Nee called him the Resident Boss. He found out that he could not pray with wine on the table. Being a young Christian, and the season for it, he had sought to give thanks with wine on the table. Unable to pray, he began to observe what might be different from the last time he prayed. Finally he realized that with the changing season wine had been made available for the first time since his conversion. He could not give thanks. The Spirit restrained him. With the removing of the wine he was able to thank God freely for the meal. In explaining later what had happened, he reported, "The Resident Boss (the Spirit of God) would not let me pray."

Third, to pray in the Spirit is to pray *in the Spirit's communion*. In the highest sense prayer is communion with God. It is in the fellowship of the Spirit. The deepest and most sacred intimacies of love both human and divine are wordless. If prayer at first seems to be on our part, the Spirit reciprocates and prayer is his part and ours. In the first stage of prayer we pray and ask God to help us. In the transcendent stage of prayer the Spirit in his temple, our body, prays in us in fellowship according to the will of God. He makes prayer more than human. He renders it supernatural! He is God the Spirit, representing God the Father and God the Son. He ever works to renew our minds. He is the power that works in us both to will and to do God's good pleasure. He is the one that unifies our hearts in prayer and makes them an irresistible unity in intercession. The *secret* of it all is by him. The *power* of it all is by him. The *joy* of it all is by him.

Therefore, let us be sure that ours is the continuing privilege of praying in the Spirit. Lord, teach us to pray!

---

1. Lehman Strauss, *Sense and Nonsense About Prayer*, p. 31.

Part 2

The Personal Prayer Life

The preceding chapters have largely dealt with the principles and precepts of prayer. At this point we begin to look at prayer from a personal and practical perspective. The following chapters will deal with practical matters pertaining to the private prayer life.

9

A Perspective on Personal Prayer

The Spirit of God needs the nature of the believer as a shrine in which to offer His intercession. "Your body is the temple of the Holy Ghost." When Jesus Christ cleansed the temple, he "would not [allow any man to carry] any vessel through the temple." The Spirit of God will not allow you to use your body for your own convenience. Jesus ruthlessly cast out all of them that sold and bought in the temple, and said, "My house shall be called the house of prayer; but ye have made it a den of thieves."

Have we recognized that our body is the temple of the Holy Ghost? (Oswald Chambers).[1]

Whatever we learn of the principles and precepts of prayer in general, it must be kept in mind that prayer in its final analysis is personal. This is not to downplay the public prayer meeting, the prayer time with the family, or praying with a prayer mate. All of these are vital but none substitute for or rise above the personal prayer life. Since perspective means much in evaluating anything, I want to share with you a personal perspective which has made prayer of more conscious value to me.

I have cherished from the time of my conversion the privilege of personal prayer and have made it a practice to develop the personal prayer life. We have been told that "familiarity breeds contempt." Perhaps that is not always true, but it certainly encourages presumption if we are not careful. We who are blessed with freedom are apt to treat it lightly and abuse it by sheer neglect. The same is true with prayer.

It helps to keep in mind that we have not always had prayer as a personal privilege as we do today. The value of anything is enhanced with the imagination of what life would be without it. So let us engage in some "sanctified imagination."

1450 B.C.

Your imagination has become a time machine which has landed you in the fifteenth century B.C. We find ourselves amid a great host of people. There is much excitement and coming and going. They seem to be taking an offering—but what a strange offering! There are heaping piles of skins of all kind, carpets, and draperies. There are other piles of rings, earrings, bracelets, and jewels of gold and silver.

Upon inquiry we discover that the Israelites are planning a building program! Now this would seem strange to anyone! Why would folks on a journey be interested in a building program? Upon closer investigation we discover that it is to be a portable tent whose dimensions had come directly from the God of heaven. He personally had designated every article that would be used in the building. He had dictated the exact dimensions and appointed the furnishings. He had even selected the architects for the job and filled them with his Spirit, giving them wisdom, understanding, and knowledge. Thus Bezaleel and Aholiab were prepared to receive the offerings and direct the building of this ingenious tabernacle in the wilderness. But from where had this immense offering come? Had not these people been slaves during their sojourn in Egypt? Yes, but God had thought of everything. Since God knows everything, he prepares for everything. He knew the need of the tabernacle and ordered the Israelites to "borrow" from the Egyptians before they left, and "borrow" they did. God gave them favor in the eyes of the Egyptians and they gave them their jewels, bracelets, earrings, draperies, carpets, and gold and silver! And how these people gave! In fact they gave too much—more than enough. So much in fact that Moses had to make an announcement to that effect and restrain them from giving more!

"But why such a tent at all?" we are moved to ask. "We will just have to move it again and again." We are informed that the tent is being constructed because God ordered it. That only satisfies us partially. Why did God order it? The simple answer is that God wanted a means to dwell among his people. He wanted to meet with his people! We must remember that the Savior had not come. There was no Bible. The purpose of the tabernacle in the wilderness was that God and man might have a meeting place.

Through the months that follow, the tabernacle begins to take shape. How unusual it is. There is no place for the congregation! The meeting house is entirely too small! It would have to be stretched to serve the prayer meeting crowd! Ah, but we have forgotten, and this is another day and another dispensation. The congregation is on the outside! Only the priestly order can come into the outer court and holy place. Only the high priest can come into the holy of holies. He must act in behalf of the people.

Finally the tent of the congregation is completed. The furniture is placed according to divine specifications. Then a strange phenomenon occurs. When the tent is completed, the lamps lighted, and the incense burned, Moses, Aaron, and his sons wash themselves at the laver between the tent and the altar. The work is finished. Then suddenly a great cloud covers the tent and the glory of the Lord fills the tabernacle. God had come down to dwell among his people. His presence would not only be the means of fellowship and communion but also the source of direction. A cloud by day and a pillar of fire by night would be our view of the greatness of God!

"But when will our time come to worship in the new tent?" we plaintively ask. "Never!" comes the terse reply. Then we learn that the place of communion is not for the congregation. We are to be represented by the priests and only one of them, the high priest, may enter where holy God dwells and meet him.

The priests are to be properly cleaned and meticulously dressed with coats, robes, girdles, ephods, and mitres. A special anointing oil is used to anoint the tent and the priests as well as the altar. Then there is a series of offerings for the priests themselves—first, a bullock, then a ram, another ram and on and on the seemingly endless process goes. "Why all this meticulous preparation?" we ask. Man is preparing to meet Holy God and all must be ready.

And so we learn the system. On a certain day of the year, one man, representing all the people, parts the ominous veil which hangs between the holy place and the holy of holies and carries in the blood of an unblemished lamb. He sprinkles blood upon the mercy seat and there through the blood meets God for those moments. Imagine it, one man among millions, one day among hundreds, a few moments only are all that are afforded to know and meet God! Personal knowledge and communion with God are unknown to the common folks. And so it will be for hundreds of years yet until THE LAMB OF GOD!

A.D. 30

"Behold the Lamb of God which taketh away the sin of the world!" is the declaration we hear as we change time zones. It is A.D. 30 and John the Baptist is heralding the coming of the Lamb! That has particular significance to us because of where we have just been. It was the blood of a lamb that was taken to the mercy seat that was a key in making atonement for the sins of the people. Now, here is word of THE LAMB, not just *another* but *THE* LAMB to end all lambs as far as a sacrificial offering is concerned. He is to take away the sins of the world! The sins of the world are hindrances between man and God. They were what the tabernacle, the priesthood, and the offerings were all about. Now here comes one to take them away! So here he is, the one of whom the prophet Isaiah said, "The Lord hath laid on him the iniquity of us all" (53:6).

A.D. 33

We are brought to a sad scene three years later. This Lamb is being slain. Jesus is on a cross positioned between two thieves. "Why this injustice?" we ask. That we might be reconciled to God and have fellowship with him. And so the crucified Lamb willfully dies for us! Surrounding his death there were multiple miracles, but the one most important for our consideration here is that which took place in the Temple. Let us join the priests at the time of the afternoon sacrifice. We are standing in the holy place and all of a sudden the great, thick veil which hangs between the holy place and holy of holies begins to tear from top to bottom! "And behold, the veil of the temple was rent in twain from the top to the bottom; and the earth did quake, and the rocks rent" (Matt. 27:51). You and I, there through the gift of imagination, look for the first time into the holy of holies where God dwells. It is open to all!

God is saying by the rent veil . . . *The job is done, the debt is paid, all are priests!* Come unto me now through Jesus Christ and fellowship with me . . . anytime, all the time, for as much time as you desire!

And my friend, from that time unto this moment we have had the privilege of entering the holy of holies to have fellowship with God through his Spirit and in the name of his Son! Jesus arose and is our high priest in the heavenlies. He comes in his Spirit and indwells every one of us who is a believer. And because of this, any of us without prior appointment, without any credentials may come to the holy of holies at any time of the day or night to spend as long as we desire, discussing anything we care to discuss! In fact what is transcendent above all this is that we do not have to go anywhere to the holy of holies. We are the holy of holies. "Ye are the temple of God" (1 Cor. 3:16). So without traveling to another destination, I can turn inward to the deepest intimacies of personal worship because of what God has provided through Jesus Christ. The death of Jesus has paid the debt; and the life of Jesus, both in heaven and in me, is the means of continuous appropriation of this priceless privilege.

Let me repeat it lest you miss it. No more sacrifices; no more priests (all of us are priests); no more rams, and lambs, and bullocks; nor an altar of sacrifice! These were figures of the True One, the Lord Jesus Christ! He alone is our priest and through him we come to the Father with no other intermediaries. "Seeing then that we have a great high priest, that is passed into the heavens, Jesus the Son of God, let us hold fast our profession" (Heb. 4:14).

"Let us therefore come boldly unto the throne (note: no longer an altar but a throne) of grace, that we may obtain mercy, and find grace to help in time of need" (v. 16).

"Having therefore, brethren, boldness to enter into the holiest by the blood of Jesus, by a new and living way, which he hath consecrated for us, through the veil, that is to say, his flesh; and having a high priest over the house of God; let us draw near with a true heart in full assurance of faith, having our hearts sprinkled from an evil conscience, and our bodies washed with pure water. Let us hold fast the profession of our faith without wavering; (for he is faithful that promised)'' (10:19–23).

The Twentieth Century

Now, do you see it? We have the name of Jesus, his blood, his standing in the court of prayer. We are the temples of God, made for worship the chiefest part of which is PRAYER! We are made to pray. We are made for prayer! The price is paid. The door is open! The invitation is clear.

Back from your long journey into the past, you see the perspective! You and I can come to pray without being announced or having to set an appointment and have audience with the God of heaven for as long as is needed. Praise the Lord!

Now, in the light of all this, do you not think it shameful how little time we spend taking advantage of the priceless privilege of prayer? Take some time just now to thank God for the open door of prayer.

---

1. Oswald Chambers, *My Utmost for His Highest* (Toronto: Dodd, Mead, and Co., 1935), 313.

10

Preparation for Personal Prayer

While we are encouraged to come before the throne of grace boldly, we are never encouraged to come thoughtlessly, or lightly, or unprepared. As surely as the priests of Moses' day needed careful preparation for divine service, so we should be careful to be certain that we come as prepared as we are bold (Author Unknown).

Many an endeavor fails because of poor preparation. One of the basic laws of prayer is that of right relationships. Getting on praying ground must be achieved if we are to pray prevailing. I suggest that you follow carefully the material in this chapter as a means of preparing to pray. I am first going to use an approach that was first used, as far as I can determine, among missionaries. It is called "Heart-searching for prayer preparation and personal revival." Then I will give you a basic outline of Psalm 139, a great chapter in preparing to pray.

Confession of sin is necessary for fellowship with God and revival among God's people. Prayerfully consider the following questions. Go through these questions one by one. Answer truthfully each question. Every yes means a sin in your life.

In reading these questions, as you are convicted of sin, confess it at once to God. Be willing to make it right, then you can claim forgiveness. First John 1:9 says, "If we confess our sins, he is faithful and just to forgive us our sins, and to cleanse us from all unrighteousness."

Be sure to name your sin to God. For example, "Lord, I have not put you first in my plans"; or "I have neglected thy Word and prayer." Do not make even the least excuse for sin of any kind in your life. "He that covereth his sin shall not prosper: but whoso confesseth and forsaketh them shall have mercy" (Prov. 28:13).

No matter what others do, or do not do, Christian, leave nothing undone on your part. God wants to work through you to bring about a great spiritual awakening. He can begin by your fulfilling every requirement shown by the Lord through the Holy Spirit and the Word. A revival from the presence of the Lord begins today . . . if you desire it! (Read the Scriptures first. Ask the question. Give a truthful answer, yes or no.)

1. Matthew 6:12,14–15—"Forgive us our debts, as we forgive our debtors. For if ye forgive men their trespasses, your heavenly Father will also forgive you: but if ye forgive not men their trespasses, neither will your Father forgive your trespasses."

Is there anyone against whom you hold a grudge? Anyone you haven't forgiven? Anyone you hate? Anyone you do not love? Are there any misunderstandings that you are unwilling to forget? Is there any person against whom you are harboring bitterness, resentment, or jealousy? Anyone you dislike to hear praised or well spoken of? Do you allow anything to justify a wrong attitude toward another?

2. Matthew 6:33—"But seek ye first the kingdom of God and his righteousness; and all these things shall be added unto you."

Is there anything in which you have failed to put God first? Have your decisions been made after your own wisdom and desires, rather than seeking and following God's will? Do any of the following in any way interfere with your surrender and service to God: Ambition, pleasures, loved ones, friendships, desire for recognition, money, your own plans?

3. Mark 16:15—"And he said unto them, Go ye into all the world, and preach the gospel to every creature."

Have you failed to seek the lost for Christ? Have you failed to witness consistently with your mouth for the Lord Jesus Christ? Has your life not shown to the lost the Lord Jesus?

4. John 13:35—"By this shall all men know that you are my disciples, if ye have love one to another." Are you secretly pleased over the misfortunes of another? Are you secretly annoyed over the

accomplishments or advancements of another? Are you guilty of any contention or strife? Do you quarrel, argue, or engage in heated discussions? Are you a partaker in any divisions, or party spirit? Are there people whom you deliberately slight?

5. Acts 20:35—"It is more blessed to give than to receive."

Have you robbed God by withholding his due of time, talents, or money? Have you given less than a tenth of your income for God's work? Have you failed to support mission work either in prayer or in offering?

6. 1 Corinthians 4:2—"Moreover it is required in stewards, that a man be found faithful."

Are you undependable so that you cannot be trusted with responsibilities in the Lord's work? Are you allowing your emotions to be stirred for things of the Lord but doing nothing about it?

7. 1 Corinthians 6:19–20—"What? know ye not that your body is the temple of the Holy Ghost which is in you, which ye have of God, and ye are not your own? For ye are bought with a price: therefore glorify God in your body, and in your spirit, which are God's."

Are you in any way careless with your body? Do you fail to care for it as the temple of the Holy Spirit? Are you guilty of intemperance in eating and drinking? Do you have any habits which are defiling to the body?

8. 1 Corinthians 10:31—"Whether therefore ye eat, or drink, or whatsoever ye do, do all to the glory of God."

Do you take the slightest credit for anything good about you, rather than give all the glory to God? Do you talk of what you have done rather than what Christ has done? Are your statements mostly about "I"? Are your feelings easily hurt? Have you made a pretense of being something that you are not?

9. Ephesians 3:20—"Now unto him that is able to do exceeding abundantly above all that we ask or think, according to the power that worketh in us."

Are you self-conscious rather than Christ-conscious? Do you allow feelings of inferiority to keep you from attempting things you should in serving God?

10. Ephesians 4:28—"Let him that stole steal no more: but rather let him labour, working with his hands the thing which is good, that he may have to give to him that needeth."

Do you underpay? Do you do very little in your work? Have you been careless in the payment of your debts? Do you waste time for yourself and for others?

11. Ephesians 4:31—"Let all bitterness, and wrath, and anger, and clamour, and evil speaking, be put away from you, with all malice."

Do you complain? Do you find fault? Do you have a critical attitude toward any person or thing? Are you irritable or cranky? Do you ever carry hidden anger? Do you get angry? Do you become impatient with others? Are you ever harsh or unkind?

12. Ephesians 5:16—"Redeeming the time, because the days are evil."

Do you listen to unedifying radio or TV programs? Do you read unworthy magazines? Do you partake in worldy amusements? Do you find it necessary to seek satisfaction from any questionable source? Are you doing certain things that show that you are not satisfied with the Lord Jesus Christ?

13. Ephesians 5:20—"Giving thanks always for all things unto God and the Father, in the name of our Lord Jesus Christ."

Have you neglected to thank him for all things, the seemingly bad as well as the good? Have you virtually called God a liar by doubting his Word? Do you worry? Is your spiritual temperature based on your feelings instead of on the facts of God's Word?

14. Philippians 1:21—"For to me to live is Christ, and to die is gain."

Are you taken up with the cares of this life? Is your conversation or heart joy over "things" rather than the Lord and His Word? Does anything mean more to you than living for and pleasing Christ?

15. Philippians 2:14—"Do all things without murmurings and disputings."

Do you ever by word or deed seek to hurt someone? Do you gossip? Do you speak unkindly concerning people when they are not present? Do you carry prejudice against true Christians because they are of some different group than yours, or because they do not see everything exactly like you?

16. Philippians 4:4—"Rejoice in the Lord always: and again I say, Rejoice."

Have you neglected to seek to be pleasing to him in all things? Do you carry any bitterness toward God? Have you complained against him in any way? Have you been dissatisfied with his provision for you? Do you have any reservations as to what you would or would not do concerning anything that might be his will? Have you disobeyed some direct leading from him?

17. Colossians 3:9—"Lie not one to another, seeing that ye have put off the old man with his deeds."

Do you engage in empty and unprofitable conversation? Do you ever lie? Do you ever exaggerate? Cheat? Steal? Carefully consider, do you overcharge?

18. 2 Timothy 2:22—"Flee also youthful lusts: but follow righteousness, faith, charity, peace, with them that call on the Lord out of a pure heart."

Do you have any personal habits that are not pure? Do you allow impure thoughts about the opposite sex to stay in your mind? Do you read that which is impure or suggests unholy things? Do you indulge in any unclean entertainment? Are you guilty of the lustful look?

19. Hebrews 10:25—"Not forsaking the assembling of ourselves together, as the manner of some is; but exhorting one another: and so much the more, as ye see the day approaching."

Do you stay away from meetings of preaching the gospel? Do you whisper or think about other things while God's Word is being read or preached? Are you irregular in attendance at services? Do you neglect to attend and participate in meetings for prayer? Have you neglected or slighted daily or private prayer? Have you neglected thanksgiving at meals? Have you neglected daily family devotions?

20. Hebrews 13:7—"Remember them which have the rule over you, who have spoken unto you the word of God: whose faith follow, considering the end of their conversation."

Do you hesitate to submit to leaders in the church or elsewhere? Are you lazy? Do you rebel at requests given to you to help in the work of the gospel? Do you in any way have a stubborn or unteachable spirit?

21. James 1:27—"Pure religion and undefiled before God and the Father is this, To visit the fatherless and widows in their affliction, and to keep himself unspotted from the world."

Have you allowed yourself to become "spotted" by the world? Is your manner of dress pleasing to God? Do you spend beyond what is pleasing to God on anything? Do you neglect to pray about the things that you buy?

22. James 4:6—"But he giveth more grace, Wherefore he saith, God resisteth the proud, but giveth grace unto the humble."

Do you feel that you have done quite well as a Christian? That you are not so bad? That you are good enough? Are you stubborn? Do you insist on having your own way? Do you insist on your own "rights"?

23. James 3:11—"Doth a fountain send forth at the same place sweet water and bitter?"

Have you dishonored him and hindered his work by criticizing his servants? Have you failed to pray regularly for your pastor and other spiritual leaders? Do you find it hard to be corrected? Is there rebellion toward one who wants to restore you? Are you more concerned about what people will think than what will be pleasing to God?

If you have been honest and true in the matter of admitting your sins, then you are ready for cleansing. Sins that are admitted are sins that are confessed.

Remember three things:

(1) If the sin is against God, confess it to God, and make things right with God.

(2) If the sin is against another person, confess it to God, and make things right with the other one.

(3) If the sin is against a group, confess it to God, and make it right with the group.

If there is full confession, there will be full cleansing. Then the joy of the Lord will follow. Then there can be testimony and prayer in the power of the Spirit. Revival will follow.

Psalm 19:12—"Who can understand his errors? Cleanse thou me from secret faults."

A Full-scale Investigation

Personal and corporate revival awaits a full-scale spiritual investigation. When we pray for revival we are praying for God to conduct a spiritual fact-finding mission. In preparation for personal prayer there needs to be a life free from sin for prayer to take place. The psalmist declared, "If I regard iniquity in my heart, the Lord will not hear me."

Having carefully read the first part of this chapter, I now ask you to take your Bible and read slowly and deliberately Psalm 139. Then, with your Bible still open beside you to Psalm 139, slowly read these pages.

Investigation is common today. We will stand for many years in the tragic shadow of the findings of the Watergate investigations. This debacle seemed to touch off a chain reaction of investigations in America. Though the findings have proved embarrassing in many instances we do well to note the unpublicized results of such investigations—the *cleansing* of the system, the *condemnation* of the guilty, the *clearing* of the just, and *confirmation* of justice.

So let us turn to Psalm 139. Please do not go on reading until you have read the entire psalm. Do it now!

Who among us does not need often to have a full-scale investigation in our lives. In this psalm are set forth the qualities of a proper investigation.

I. There Must Be a Confidence in the Investigator.
   A. The reaches of his intelligence (vv. 1–6)
      1. Past knowledge (v. 1)
      2. Present positions and locations (vv. 2–3)
      3. Word and thoughts (vv. 2–4)
   B. The realms of his influence (vv. 7–12)
      1. Heaven and hell (v. 8)
      2. Remote isles of the sea (vv. 9–10)
      3. Darkness (vv. 11–12)
   C. The rightness of his intentions (vv. 13–20)
      1. God presided over my birth (v. 13)
      2. God purposes my life (vv. 14–18)
      3. God punishes the wicked (vv. 19–20)
II. There Must Be a Call to Be Investigated.
   A. A personal commitment against the wickedness (vv. 21–22)
   B. A personal investigation called for (v. 23.)
   C. A pervasive investigation called for (Know my *heart* and *thoughts*, v. 23.)
   D. A purposeful investigation called for (To see if there be any wicked way in me, v. 24.)
III. There Must Be a Commitment to Abide by the Investigation's Findings.
   A. A personal commitment (Lead *me*, v. 24b.)
   B. A permanent commitment (In the way *everlasting*, v. 24.)

The psalmist has here presented the *route to revival*. Will you go to God in prayer just now with the closing words of that great Psalm? "Search me, O God, and know my heart: try me and know my thoughts: and see if there be any wicked way in me, and lead me in the way everlasting."

11

The Personal Prayer Life

*"You tell us what we should do, but you do not tell us how!"
is the charge often levelled at those of us who preach and
teach. I greatly fear, for the greater part, that our plea shall
have to be "Guilty, as charged!" The enemy does not care
how much you read about prayer or how much you know about
it if he can keep you from the practice of it. With these facts in
mind you will notice fundamental and practical suggestions set
forth in both preceding and following pages (J. R. T.).*

*I care not what black spiritual crisis we may come through
or what delightful spiritual Canaan we may enter, no blessing
of the Christian life becomes continually possessed unless we
are men and women of regular, daily, unhurried, secret linger-
ings in prayer (Sidlow Baxter).*

*The Master never asks of us such labor as shall leave no
leisure to sit at his feet (Source Unknown).*

*What a man is, he is alone on his knees before God, and no
more! (Robert Murray McCheyne).*

More than 10 percent of the Sermon on the Mount has to do with
prayer. The greater part of that material on prayer is seen in Matthew
6:5–13, with the last five verses covering the Model Prayer. The
remainder of the emphases on prayer are in Matthew 7:7–11.

Though Jesus was talking to the whole group of disciples, the
emphasis here is on the personal prayer life. In verse 6 there is an
interesting shift from plural in the previous verse to singular here.

"But thou (singular) when thou prayest, enter into thy (singular) closet, and when thou (singular) hast shut thy (singular) door, pray to thy (singular) Father which is in secret; and thy Father which seeth in secret shall reward thee (singular) openly." Now this is vital in that Jesus was making clear that the central thrust of prayer was in private life. No amount of public or corporate praying will compensate for the lack of personal prayer. Jesus here gives us four valid facets of the personal prayer life, the *time*, the *place*, the *manner*, and the *results*.

The Time of Prayer

Three times Jesus says, "When you pray." This is an assumption that his disciples will pray. People of all religions pray. The Pharisees prayed. There is a sense in which this assumption of Jesus is stronger than a command. Thus with the assumption repeated three times in verses 5–7 leads normally to the command in verse 9, "After this manner therefore pray ye."

There are definite implications in this passage which bring light to us regarding personal prayer. The first is that there is to be a *regular* time of prayer. It is valid to engage in prayer by the way. There is no way or reason to depreciate what I call "snatch time" praying. We are to be always in prayer as far as attitude is concerned. But nothing will take the place of the *regular* time of prayer daily. The private prayer time is the key to the whole of the prayer life. I have noticed that there is much information in many books on the *principles* of prayer in general but very little on the *practice* of prayer in the personal life. No one told me of the importance of a daily quiet time at the time of my conversion. The cost of the lack of the knowledge of its importance is inestimable! "When" is an adverb suggesting a time. The verbs in this passage are in the present tense denoting *continuing* action.

The second implication regarding time is found in the Model Prayer, commonly called the "Lord's Prayer." Jesus said, "Give us this day our daily bread" (Matt. 6:11). Notice two things; first, the nature of the prayer is *daily*, that is it is to be regular; second, it looks out upon the day from the morning. It is not likely that one would be praying this particular prayer at the close of the day. Thus, it is far more than a suspicion or an assumption that Jesus was here suggesting that his disciples have a regular prayer time and that in the morning. I must here add my own personal testimony. I have found it very difficult for years to arise in the morning. Had there been a better time to meet God in prayer and communion I would have found it! I confess that as much as I love the sleep of the early morning hours, I have had to choose this time as the most precious time of prayer.

The Place of Prayer

Jesus here simply suggests the "closet." The same word is translated in Matthew 24:26 as "secret chamber." Without laboring what may seem a small point, let me suggest to you that it is vital that you have a *place* of prayer. Your prayer life will suffer until you mark a place where life's greatest business will be carried on. There are three brief suggestions inherent in this command, in verse six, "When thou prayest, enter into thy closet, and when thou hast shut the door, pray . . ." First, there is to be a *set* place. Prayer is to be continuous and the place is to be singularly designated. Second, it is to be a *secluded* place. Such is the suggestion of the word used here. This is important. The one who prays should not be hindered by lack of privacy. Isolation should be stated among the valid laws of personal prayer. Third, it is to be a *shut* place. "When thou hast shut your door . . ." is an important consideration in prayer. A shut door is a sign of apartness, aloneness, exclusion, and seclusion. There is something comforting about being "shut in" with the Lord.

The Manner of Prayer

This is not the place for an exhaustive study of the model prayer. However, I do want you to see that the key word is "manner." Jesus did not say, "Pray this." He said, "Pray after this manner." I want you to see the difference. Had he said, "Pray this," we would be justified in quoting this prayer and feeling that we have prayed. But the truth is that one may quote this prayer without having prayed. For this prayer, strangely, but certainly, demands a certain disposition of the one praying it. What Jesus was saying was this: "Pray with this attitude, from this disposition, in this spirit." The emphasis is on "how" and not "what." Allow me to show you what I mean in the following breakdown:

Our Father.—We are praying as children of the Father, recognizing all the saved as brothers and sisters. If there are breaches of fellowship resulting from our actions and feelings, we believe the spirit of our praying. "Our" is a word which recognizes corporate family relationship.

Which art in heaven, Hallowed be thy name.—This prefaces all prayer with praise and adoration. These form the doorway or entrance into prayer. This is a recognition of God's exalted position and God's *excellent* name. Thus, we come not only as children but as *adoring* children.

Thy kingdom come, Thy will be done in earth, as it is in heaven.—One cannot get past this point in the prayer without bowing to lordship. Why should we pray for his will to be done and his kingdom come in earth as in heaven unless that has already been a personal experience in our own lives? This portion of the model prayer demands on the part of the one praying a yieldedness to the King of kings and a commitment to his will. For this reason I do not often encourage public repetitions of this prayer. I may be cooperating with a spirit of deceit in which someone is led to say something they do not at all mean.

Give us this day our daily bread.—This implies a satisfaction with no more than a day's supply and delight with the fact of daily dependence upon the hand of God for provision. To worry about tomorrow and to pray this prayer today is sheer hypocrisy.

And forgive us our debts as we forgive our debtors.—The unspoken assertion of the one who prays this prayer is, "I have forgiven all!" If one has not, he has no business praying this prayer. In fact, if there is unforgiveness in one's heart, this is a prayer inviting God's unforgiveness. The words are "Forgive us as (just like, in the same manner) we forgive our debtors."

And lead us not into temptation, but deliver us from evil.—This is the prayer of one who has become aware of his own weakness. He further has become aware of the power of sin. To stand in the disposition of this prayer is to be committed to cooperating with God in avoiding situations where temptation is suspect. I have no business praying this prayer and at the same time being in the habit of deliberately walking in temptation alley. Here we look Godward, never manward, for our deliverance from evil.

For thine is the kingdom, and the power, and the glory, for ever. Amen.—Here is the acknowledgement that everything is God's. Here the one praying puts himself completely into God's hands giving all ownership, authority, and glory to him FOREVER!

Now, look back over the model prayer. Examine your life in the light of the implications. As you repeat aloud the words, phrase by phrase, take a moment to observe the disposition suggested in each phrase. You will find the *model* then becoming *meaningful* indeed.

The Result of Prayer

We pray in secret. God sees in secret. But the results of prayer are not secret! "Thy Father which seeth in secret shall reward thee openly" (Matt. 6:6). I can promise you, my friend, no investment you will ever make will have more immediate and permanent rewards than that of personal prayer. Who can describe the magnitude of those rewards he promises? The word here translated "reward" is the word which literally means "to give back." Prayer is reciprocal. We give to God; he gives back to us. What an exchange!

12

Procedures in the Personal Prayer Life

If the experience of reading this volume does not move the reader to studiously begin or seriously improve his or her personal program of prayer, its central objective will be lost and for that particular reader this work will have been in vain. It is, as suggested earlier, a volume designed to leave you praying. A vitalization of the personal prayer life will touch the whole of the prayer life, in family, church, and other cases of group praying. The reader may wonder why this emphasis on the daily period of prayer and worship. It is because this is the starting point of all prayer on the human side. In the "Perspective" I said, "No believer's prayer life will rise to stay above the level of his or her personal, regular, daily time of worship with God." It is toward the establishing, maintaining, and enhancing of this endeavor that these suggestions are given.

What follows here is a series of practical, down-to-earth, almost kindergarten suggestions relating to the personal prayer time.

1. Establish in your heart and mind the priority of the personal prayer time. You will find yourself doing what you consider important. You will spend in an average twenty-four hour period about seven hours sleeping as well as a couple of hours eating. That is a total of nine hours. Why? Because it is absolutely essential to your physical well-being! Through the years you have established these things as priorities. Jesus prayed much and often. He arose a great while before it was day and sought the Father. He prayed all night on occasion. Set your mind as to prayer's importance and ask God to enforce your choice to give him time. The record bears out that praying men were useful men.

CHARLES SIMEON devoted the hours of from four to eight in the morning to God.

MARTIN LUTHER said, "If I fail to spend two hours in prayer each morning, the devil gets the victory through the day. I have so much business I cannot get on without three hours daily in prayer."

BISHOP ASBURY said, "I propose to rise at four o'clock as often as I can and spend two hours in prayer and meditation."

JOSEPH ALLEINE arose at four o'clock for his business of praying until eight. If he heard other tradesmen plying their business before he was up, he would exclaim, "Oh, how this shames me! Doth not my Master deserve more than theirs?"

ADONIRAM JUDSON suggested, "Arrange thy affairs, if possible, so that thou canst leisurely devote two or three hours every day not merely to devotional exercises but to the very act of secret prayer and communion with God."

I have recalled for you those who have distinguished themselves as what some term "extreme" cases to encourage you as to prayer's priority.

2. Designate a time and a place for your prayer time. An ideal private place may be well nigh impossible to some. I encourage you to set a place, even if it is not ideal at the outset. If you will begin God will undertake to provide the necessary privacy.

3. Begin to protect your sleep time with a view to the early-morning prayer time. In other words, go to bed at a proper time. This is an acquired habit. I have heard myself say, "I am a night person." I have had to admit, however, that this is more of a habit acquired than a trait inherited.

4. Devise a feasible means of awakening every morning. May I suggest an electric alarm clock placed across the room! The reasons for both object and location are obvious I am sure!

5. When you wake up, get up! The battle of the blankets will never be won from the underneath side. There is a twilight zone between sleeping and waking in which the faculties of mind, emotions, and will are greatly impaired. This seems to vary in degree in different people. Don't just lie there, GET UP!

6. When you get up, bounce up. I mean get up with determination. Be serious about it. Every second of hesitation is critical.

7. When you get up, and bounce up, do whatever it takes to get wide awake. Run in place, jump up and down, or splash water in your face. This is a good time to do some light physical exercises. Clear your brain, you have an important appointment coming up!

8. When you get up, fix up. I find it very helpful to dress for whatever demands the day makes upon me before my prayer time. The interval of time occupied with fixing up is a time of reflection, praise, and anticipation.

9. Take your prayer equipment with you to the place of prayer. A Bible, prayer notebook, note pad, and a daily devotional book will prove to be helpful equipment in your prayer time. I have been using for some time an intercessory prayer plan notebook devised by Peter Lord, pastor of Park Avenue Baptist Church of Titusville, Florida. Its designation, after a recent revision and improvement, is The 2959 Plan. It will be self-explanatory to the user. I recommend above all others the use of the daily devotional book, *My Utmost for His Highest.* There are other good ones; to me this one is best.

The preceding procedures have dealt with the matters of preparing to pray. The following have to do with procedures within the prayer time itself.

10. Open your Bible, asking God to bless the reading of the Word with concentration and understanding. Remember that this time of Bible reading is not necessarily for the purpose of preparing for teaching or preaching responsibilities, but for preparation in prayer. I read five psalms every day and have proposed to read a chapter from the book of Proverbs. There are many times, such as this morning, when I felt the urgent need to fortify myself with some other passages on the believer's warfare and weapons. I have read the Psalms every month for the past few years and testify to you that they are still coming alive in my heart.

I will discuss with you some vital exercises with the use of the Bible in your prayer life in a subsequent chapter entitled "The Word of God and Personal Prayer."

11. If you choose to use a devotional book, read a daily segment from it at this time. Many have been the times when Oswald Chambers was used to say something that struck a responsive chord in my needy heart. And it ceaselessly amazes me that the particular day in the book, *My Utmost for His Highest,* had just the right message for me!

12. I have found it helpful on many occasions simply to write God a love letter. This is one reason for the note pad or spiral-ring notebook in addition to your prayer notebook.

13. Begin your actual time of prayer with thanksgiving and praise. Thanksgiving is simply enumerating those things for which you are grateful while praise is the pouring out of the heart in adoration to God. We will further discuss this secret of getting into prayer in Part III. I have a number of pages designated as praises in my prayer notebook. Most of them are taken from the Psalms. I also have found many songs in the hymnal to be written unto the Lord and are effective praise songs.

14. Form a daily prayer list. It is at this point where I usually go to my daily prayer list in my prayer notebook. I have a page for each name and almost every day I record my prayer or perhaps an answer to a prayer next to the date under the name. This list is growing and will need to be revised later because of its size. I have the names of my family first, my President, and other prayer commitments following. I will specify later how I pray for these on occasion using specific Scripture verses. I may simply mention a name to the Lord and little more. I may stop and specifically ask the Lord to give me a special impression of the prayer need of that person or I may choose to use a prayer from the Word such as, "And this I pray, that your love may bound yet more and more in knowledge and in all judgment" (Phil. 1:9).

15. You will need to formulate a weekly prayer list. You will soon have too many people and matters for which to pray daily. Your 2959 PLAN will have daily dividers in it for each day of the week (aside from a "daily" divider). Here is the way I have divided my weekly prayer list:

SUNDAY	My church and its staff The lost
MONDAY	The missionaries. . . . It has been my privilege to visit many of our mission fields. I have the names of missionaries in these fields in my prayer book.
TUESDAY	The Southern Baptist Convention, its agencies, schools, seminaries, leadership, etc.

WEDNESDAY   This is a day for personal examination in areas such as disciplines, attitudes, family relationships, Bible study, etc.

THURSDAY   This is a day of praise. My verse for this day is Psalm 119:164, "Seven times a day do I praise thee [Lord] because of thy righteous judgments." I seek to allow praise to pervade the day in a special way.

FRIDAY   This day is for praying for a number of people and matters, friends, etc.

SATURDAY   A special day to pray for the schedule to which I am committed as well as churches where I have been. A good time to remember backslidden believers.

16. There should always be a time when we pray regarding urgent matters of current attention. If form is allowed to dictate the prayer life, it will weaken. But we will do best what we plan best.

17. I have a place in my prayer book for long-standing, contingent matters. It may be a situation of concern, one on which I am waiting for spiritual light, or a matter in which I have agreed to be a partner in prayer with someone else.

18. You may want to have, as I have, a special place of attention for those who are your intercessors.

19. I suggest that you have a prayer list of those who have spoken against you. I began to do this several years ago. Let me suggest several considerations at this point: First, they may not have said it. Second, what they said may have credibility. Third, they may already be sorry that they said it. None of these may be true; but regardless, it is never a mistake to pray for them until there is nothing but love present in your heart for them.

20. I suggest a page entitled "Rehearsing the Truth." On this page I have written statements which refer to my position as a child of God based on the Word. There are times when I feel that I need to simply rehearse these facts to saturate my mind. I will enlarge on this in the next chapter.

21. A checklist for prayer armor will help! I have noticed when flying with private pilots their use of a checklist. I have a page in my prayer book on which I have listed the armor, piece by piece. This is usually before I pray and when I am sensitive that there is going to be some warfare in the prayer experience.

22. There are certain prayers that you may want to write down to have for later reference. I have noticed today in going through my prayer book a prayer that the Lord gave me when I was praying for something without an answer. "Lord, I praise you for who you are! You are the high and lofty one who inhabits eternity whose name is holy. You do as you please and you are pleased with what you do. If you can do anything and choose not to do a thing for which I ask, I can as wisely thank you for not doing it as much as for doing it. Your delay means that you may want to alter my desire, give me my desire later, or give me something better than I know how to desire. Thank you, Lord, for what you have not done!" I have often run across this prayer with blessing at a strategic time.

23. I suggest a listing and memorization of specific prayer promises from the Word. These serve to fortify our faith as God personalizes them to our heart.

24. Revise the shape of your prayer list every few months. Keep it fresh. When you sense that a part of your prayer time is dragging, ask the Lord to impress you with what you need to do to enliven it.

25. I suggest that in your private prayer time you pray aloud when this is possible. I have found that when I pray aloud my thoughts tend to stay on track better than when praying silently. The psalmist said, "Evening, and morning, and at noon, will I pray, and cry aloud: and he shall hear my voice (Ps. 55:17). Jesus must have prayed aloud because his prayer in John 17 is recorded. He undoubtedly spoke his prayers. Matthew records that "He fell on his face and prayed, saying . . ." (26:39). It is also wise to read the Scripture aloud even when you are alone. You receive it twice when you do, once through the eyes, and again through the ears. After reading the Scripture, it will seem natural to slip into audible prayer. If you are having problems with the idea of praying publicly, these suggestions will be especially helpful. As you become familiar with the sound of your own voice in prayer, it will seem natural in the presence of others and you will not be self-conscious.

There are many other suggestions that could be made but we will leave off for now. I am asked questions about such matters as thanksgiving, praise, and meditation. Rather than make them in the form of suggestions, I am going to discuss them more fully in later chapters.

At this point you should be putting into action some of these suggestions in your personal prayer time. I would be delighted if you would put my name and ministry somewhere on your prayer list!

13

The Word of God and Personal Prayer

The Word of God is the fulcrum upon which the lever of prayer is placed, and by which things are mightily moved. God has committed himself, his purpose, and his promise to prayer. His Word become the basis, the inspiration of our praying, and there are circumstances under which, by importunate prayer, we may obtain an addition, or an enlargement of his promises.

Prayer is the great theme and content of the Bible's message to mankind. It is the basis, the directory of the prayer of faith (E. M. Bounds).[1]

Thou hast magnified thy word above all thy name (Ps. 138:2).

My soul cleaveth unto the dust; quicken thou me according to thy word (Ps. 119:25).

And take . . . the sword of the Spirit, which is the word of God: praying always with all prayer and supplication (Eph. 6:17–18).

We see three things from these Scriptures. First, in Psalm 138:2 we see God's attitude and standing with regard to his Word. I must admit to you that this is to me a startling passage! I have sought the original language and commentaries and have come to one conclusion. It means what it says! The Bible is the Word of God but the psalmist, in this statement, could not have been referring to the Bible as we have it today. We can surely, however, believe that God has presided over and preserved the message he intended to come to us and that the Bible is certainly included in this blessed statement now!

The word used here for "word," means promise. God has made promises and has chosen to exalt his faithfulness to those promises above the level of the exaltation of his own name. His name stands for the whole manifestation of himself. This simply means that if his Word fails, his name fails. God is inextricably committed to keep his Word. This is simply to say that God's Word stands because God stands by his Word. It will greatly aid our praying if we will stand where God stands with regard to his Word.

Second, in Psalm 119:25, we see the effect of the Word upon man. It quickens, makes alive. It brings alive hope and provides the vital forces needed for prayer. It is there that we discover radiant promises and abounding hope. What happens when we read the Word of God? We are enlivened, that is, we are made alive to God. Listen to the manner in which the psalmist magnifies the Word in Psalm 19:7–8: "The law of the Lord is perfect, converting the soul: the testimony of the Lord is sure, making wise the simple. The statutes of the Lord are right, rejoicing the heart: the commandment of the Lord is pure, enlightening the eyes."

What results we may expect from the Word of God! This is the reason that the enemy is making an all-out attempt to discredit the Word of God. If he can discredit it in our thinking, we then have no valid basis for praying prevailingly and expectantly.

Third, we see the use of the Word of God in the warfare. It is the sword of the Spirit, our offensive weapon. At this point I want to share with you something that I have only recently discovered about this passage. There are two words which are translated as "word" in the Bible. One is *logos* and the other is *rhema*. W. E. Vine in his *Expository Dictionary of New Testament Word* says, "The significance of *rhema* as distinct from *logos* is exemplified in the injunction to take 'the sword of the Spirit, which is the Word *(rhema)* of God,' Ephesians 6:17; here the reference is not to the whole Bible as such, but to the individual Scripture which the Spirit brings to our remembrance for use in time of need, a prerequisite being the regular storing of the mind with Scripture."

Now this is tremendously significant for our study as well as in all other areas of truth. The Bible becomes a double blessing in that it is the record of what God has said. That is the *logos*. Further, as the Holy Spirit moves in us as we study the Word, he individualizes certain promises and claims and the *logos* becomes *rhema!* It is not the Bible as a tangible entity that prepares us for warfare and defeats the devil. It is that truth made real by the Holy Spirit and activated through our lives that defeats him. There are other references which are enhanced by the use of the word *rhema*. Luke 1:37 says in the King James Version, "For with God nothing shall be impossible." The literal rendering is: "No Word of God [*rhema*] shall be without power!" In other words, what God individualizes through his written Word to you, making it the RHEMA, will have power. There is another worth mentioning here. Romans 10:17 says, "So then faith comes by hearing, and hearing by the word of God." The word here is *rhema*. One can read the Bible for years and yet not have faith. The reference here is to that work of the Holy Spirit to take the written Word and make it the living Word in our hearts. It must be remembered that the source of the *rhema* is the *logos* stored in the heart and saturated through the life. You have had the experience of knowing a promise of the Scripture by memory and then having it come alive in a situation of need. It became *yours* in a manner as never before. It became *rhema*. Information had become revelation to your heart. It is through prayer that the written Word *(logos)* becomes the living Word *(rhema)* in our lives. The accuracy then of the written word becomes actuality in spiritual realities through the *rhema.*

Before we move to some uses of the Word of God in prayer, let me suggest a helpful exercise. Hold your right hand open before your face. Imagine that each of your four fingers is labeled from right to left, thusly: *Read* the Bible, *Hear* the Bible, *Study* the Bible, and *Memorize* the Bible. These are four suggested things you can do with the Bible. Now, you have a thumb left. Label it *Meditation*. Now, pick up the Bible nearest you, holding it firmly in that right hand. Now, notice that it is through reading, hearing, studying, memorizing, and meditation that you get a *grip* on the Bible. Just as that is true with the symbol of your hand holding the Bible, it will prove true in your spiritual grasp!

Prayer and the Bible go together. Without the Bible prayer has no direction. Without prayer the Bible has no dynamic. God speaks to man in the Bible. Man speaks to God in prayer. Man reads the Bible to discover God's will; he prays in order to receive the power to do

God's will. We have already observed the conditional promise of Jesus regarding His words, "If ye abide in me, and my words abide in you, ye shall ask what ye will, and it shall be done unto you" (John 15:7).

Now, let us turn to some uses of the Word in the personal prayer life.

Using the Word to Put on the Armor

Often, as I come to I sense that I am arriving at the battlefront, walking on a battlefield. When I am especially sensitive of this, I know that I need to be aware of my armor, the wardrobe for spiritual warfare. While we are always dressed in the whole armor which is none other than Christ himself, we are not always aware of the armor. "Putting on the armor" is to accept the fact and existence of the armor. I find it refreshing and reassuring to go through the exercise of imagining that the armor is visible and tangible and putting it on, piece by piece from head to toe. I personalize the Bible, putting a personal pronoun where ever it will fit. Let me illustrate, according to Ephesians 6:10–18 (author's paraphase):

I choose now to be strong in the Lord and in the power of his might. I confess that I am *in* the Lord and thus am located in the power of his might.

I choose to put on the whole armor that God has provided me, in order that I may stand against the methods of the enemy. I know that the battle is not with flesh and blood but against principalities, powers, rulers of darkness, and spiritual wickedness in high places.

Therefore I stand to accept the armor which is mine in Jesus. (I may even physically stand while doing this.) I put on the breastplate of righteousness, the Lord Jesus Christ. He is made unto me righteousness. I am made righteous in him.

I put on the girdle of truth. I accept the fact that Jesus is Truth and that Truth has made me free. I refuse deception and accept the truth.

I slip into the footwear of preparation in the Gospel. I am now ready to walk with Him.

I put on the helmet of salvation. The certainty of my salvation covers and protects my mind and my outlook. I stand in that certainty now!

I take up the shield of faith. I now trust in the trustworthiness of God! I am covered from head to toe so that Satan's fiery darts cannot touch me. (The word for shield originally referred to the stone which covered the entrance of a cave; later it was in reference to a large shield, large and oblong, covering the whole soldier's person!)

I now take my offensive weapon, the Word of God (holding up the Bible), declaring it to be true, without error, reliable, powerful and alive, God's Word to me!

And ow, I am dressed from head to foot for battle. On my head is the helmet of salvation, on my body are the breastplate of righteousness and the girdle of truth. On my feet is the footwear of preparation of the Gospel of peace. In my left hand is the shield of faith. In my right hand is the Word of God. I am now ready for the engagement of prayer.

At this point a battle-cry is in order: "I will sing unto the Lord for he hath triumphed gloriously. The Lord is my Strength and my song and he is become my salvation: he is my God, and I will prepare for him a habitation: My Father's God, and I will exalt him. The Lord is a man of war, the Lord is his name!" (Ex. 15:1–3).

If you have difficulty believing that such an exercise is valid, I suggest the next time you sense some real warfare in prayer, you try it.

Using the Word to Rehearse the Truth

The Bible fortifies us with truth to be used in the battle against the enemy. It, being truth, is true all the time, but like a sword in the scabbard, is useless until gripped firmly in the hand of faith and wielded in battle. Thus we need to believe and speak the Word in prayer. I find that the chief work of the devil is to isolate me from the continuing consciousness that I am in Jesus. If somehow he can get me to the point in my mentality that I am unaware of the glory of having Christ in me and being, myself, in him, the enemy can defeat me.

I have made the delightful discovery that I have the right to say anything about myself that God has said about me in his Word! Therefore, as a friend of mine is accustomed to doing, I can put the letters "F.M." and "A.M." by every Scripture pertaining to the saints. When I read that Scripture and see the letters "F.M.," I assert that it is *FOR ME*. The letters "A.M." remind me that since it is FOR ME I can claim it as *ALL MINE!*

I have pages in my prayer notebook entitled simply, "Rehearsing the Truth." Across the years I have listed there certain Scriptures that pertain to my position and welfare as a child of God in a personalized manner. It has been a great blessing again and again to rehearse these truths aloud as I prepare to pray. Let me illustrate (Author's para-phase):

I now confess in agreement with God that. . . .

I have been delivered from the power of darkness and translated into the Kingdom of God's Son, the Lord Jesus Christ (Col. 1:13).

I have been crucified with Christ, nevertheless I live, yet not I, but Christ lives in me, and the life I now live, I live by the faith of the Son of God who loved me and gave himself for me (Gal. 2:20).

I have received the promise of the Spirit through faith (Gal. 3:14).

My body is the temple of the Holy Spirit and he this moment indwells me, being the means by which I can claim that Jesus in me is my hope of glory (1 Cor. 3:16; Col. 1:27).

I am one with Jesus Christ. He is in me and I am in him. As he is so am I in this world. I, in all that I am, belong to him; and he, in all that he is, belongs to me (John 17:21–23; 1 John 4:17; 1 Cor. 3:21–23).

I am chosen to be holy and without blame before him in love and have acceptance with the beloved, having redemption, through his blood, the forgiveness of sins, according to the riches of his grace (Eph. 1:4, 7–8).

I have obtained an inheritance which cannot be disannulled, mine by the promises of God (Gal. 3:15–18).

I have been raised to sit with Christ in heavenly places, far above every principality, power, might, and dominion and every name that is named in this world and in the world that is to come. Nothing under Jesus' feet is over my head and all things are under his feet (Eph. 1:19 to 2:5).

I am his workmanship, created in Christ Jesus unto good works, which God hath before ordained that I should walk in them (Eph. 2:10).

I have been foreknown, predestinated, called, justified, and glorified. I am being conformed to the image of Jesus, the Son of God. All things are now working together toward this perfect goal. I can then stand and say, "If God be for me, who can be against me?" (Rom. 8:28–31).

I have boldness and access by faith in him (Eph. 3:12).

I have this treasure (HIMSELF) in earthen vessels that the excellency of the power may be of God and not of me (2 Cor. 4:7).

My God is now supplying all my need according to his riches in glory by Christ Jesus (Phil. 4:19).

I can do all things through Christ who keeps on pouring his strength through me (Phil. 4:13).

God is able to make all grace abound toward me, that I, always having all sufficiency in all things, may abound unto every good work (2 Cor. 9:8).

I am confident that he who began a good work in me will perform it, complete it to the day of Christ. (Phil. 1:3).

I am strengthened with all might according to his glorious power unto all patience and longsuffering with joyfulness (Col. 1:11).

Now friend, I assure you that after moments of confession like this when the truth of God has been rehearsed before him and in the hearing of the hosts of hell, some real praying is about to take place! These are only a few verses remarking of our rights and standings. There are dozens more! Find them, embrace them, memorize them and use them in the engagement of prayer.

Using the Word to Pray for Others

I have found in the Bible countless treasures of "ready-made" prayers. As I learn them by memory, I find that the Lord often brings them to mind as I pray for others. The advantage these prayers have over others is that there is no doubt as to the standing of such a prayer with God. When the Spirit brings it to our remembrance, we do not even have to preface it with the words, "If it be thy will." The Bible contains the will of God. When we pray according to the Word, we are praying according to his will. When we pray according to his will, he hears, and we have the petition which we requested (1 John, 5:14–15). As I go through the Bible I glean these "pre-sanctified" prayers for later use in prayer for others.

This morning as I prayed for my wife I confessed according to Isaiah 50:4–5, "The Lord God hath given me (Barbara) the tongue of the learned, that I (she) should know how to speak a word in season to him that is weary: he wakeneth morning by morning, he awakeneth mine (her) ear as the learned. The Lord God hath opened mine (her) ear, and I (she) was not rebellious, neither turned away back."

As I prayed for my daughter, the Lord gave me this confession, "This day is holy unto the Lord; mourn not, nor weep: . . . neither be ye sorry; for the joy of the Lord is Tammy's strength" (Neh. 8:9–10).

As I prayed for my son, I stood in Psalm 1, declaring "Blessed is Timmy, who walks not in the counsel of the ungodly, nor standeth in the way of sinners, nor sits in the seat of the scornful. But Timmy's delight will be in the law of the Lord and in that law will Timmy meditate day and night. He shall be like a tree planted by the rivers of water, that bringeth forth his fruit in his season; his leaf also shall not wither; and whatsoever Timmy does will prosper" (Ps. 1:1–3).

I have been often moved to pray this prayer for someone. "O that thou wouldst bless them indeed and enlarge their coast, and that thine hand might be with them, and that thou wouldst keep them from evil that it might not grieve them." This is the prayer that Jabez prayed for himself in 1 Chronicles 4:10. The final statement in the tenth verse is: "And God granted him that which he requested." What a prayer to pray for your minister or someone in the service of the Lord.

You can find prayers in the Bible that will fit all ages. Here is one for a person who is getting old, "They shall be fat and flourishing; to show that the Lord is upright: he is my rock, and there is no unrighteousness in him" (Ps. 92:14–15).

Another prayer that would fit a person growing older is in Psalm 71:18, "Now also when I am old and greyheaded, O God, forsake me not; until I have shewed thy strength unto this generation, and thy power unto everyone that is to come."

The prayers of Paul are freighted with richness. Here are some of them. Fit them to someone you know who needs such praying.

Ephesians 1:15–23—"Wherefore I also, after I heard of your faith in the Lord Jesus, and love unto all the saints, Cease not to give thanks for you, making mention of you in my prayers, That the God of our Lord Jesus Christ, the Father of glory, may give unto you the spirit of wisdom and revelation in the knowledge of him: The eyes of your understanding being enlightened; that ye may know what is the hope of his calling, and what the riches of the glory of his inheritance in the saints, And what is the exceeding greatness of his power to us-ward who believe, according to the working of his mighty power, Which he wrought in Christ, when he raised him from the dead, and set him at his own right hand in the heavenly places, Far above all principality, and power, and might, and dominion, and every name that is named, not only in this world, but also in that which is to come: And hath put all things under his feet, and gave him to be head over all things to the church, Which is his body, the fulness of him that filleth all in all."

Ephesians 3:14–19—"For this cause I bow my knees unto the Father of our Lord Jesus Christ, Of whom the whole family in heaven and earth is named, That he would grant you, according to the riches of his glory, to be strengthened with might by his Spirit in the inner man; That Christ may dwell in your hearts by faith; that ye, being rooted and grounded in love, May be able to comprehend with all the saints what is the breadth, and length, and depth, and height; And to know the love of Christ, which passeth knowledge, that ye might be filled with all the fulness of God."

Philippians 1:9–11—"And this I pray, that your love may abound yet more and more in knowledge and in all judgment; That ye may approve things that are excellent; that ye may be sincere and without offence till the day of Christ; Being filled with the fruits of righteousness, which are by Jesus Christ, unto the glory and praise of God."

Colossians 1:9–10—"For this cause we also, since the day we heard it, do not cease to pray for you, and to desire that ye might be filled with the knowledge of his will in all wisdom and spiritual understanding; That ye might walk worthy of the Lord unto all pleasing, being fruitful in every good work, and increasing in the knowledge of God."

First Thessalonians 1:2–3—"We give thanks to God always for you all, making mention of you in our prayers; Remembering without ceasing your work of faith, and labour of love, and patience of hope in our Lord Jesus Christ, in the sight of God our Father."

These meaningful verses can be turned into a benediction for someone: "Now God himself and our Father, and our Lord Jesus Christ, direct our way into you. And the Lord make you to increase and abound in love one toward another, and toward all men, even as we do toward you: To the end he may establish your hearts unblameable in holiness before God, even our Father, at the coming of our Lord Jesus Christ with all his saints" (1 Thess. 3:11–13).

Here is a fantastic prayer for anyone: "And the very God of peace sanctify you wholly; and I pray God your whole spirit and soul and body be preserved blameless unto the coming of our Lord Jesus Christ. Faithful is he that calleth you, who also will do it" (1 Thess. 5:23).

You can have confidence in praying a prayer like this: "Wherefore also we pray always for you, that our God would count you worthy of this calling, and fulfil all the good pleasure of his goodness, and the work of faith with power: That the name of our Lord Jesus Christ may be glorified in you, and ye in him, according to the grace of our God and the Lord Jesus Christ'' (2 Thess. 1:11–12).

The prayer of Jesus in John 17:1–26 affords a mine of wealth in giving us words to pray for others:

"And these things I speak in the world, that they might have my joy fulfilled in themselves'' (v.13).

"I pray not that thou shouldest take them out of the world, but that thou shouldest keep them from the evil. Sanctify them through thy truth: thy word is truth'' (vv.15,17).

"That they all may be one; as thou, Father, art in me, and I in thee, that they also may be one in us, that the world may believe that thou hast sent me'' (v.21).

"Father, I will that they also, who thou hast given me, be with me where I am; that they may behold my glory which thou hast given me'' (v.24).

Prayers like these can touch yet unborn civilizations! This whole prayer in John seventeen is still being answered and is for us. "Neither pray I for these alone, but for them also which shall believe on me through their word'' (John 17:20).

Praying the Word is a habit you will always be glad that you started. It will facilitate and enhance your memorization of the Word. Remember, the Holy Spirit can only bring those words out of the storehouse of your memory that have been put there by reading, study, hearing, memorization, and meditation. Our watchword should include, "Pray the Word!'' as it does "Preach the Word!''

Using the Word in Praise

One of the most neglected facets of worship is that of praise. Hear what the Word itself says about praise:

"It is a good thing to give thanks unto the Lord, and to sing praises unto thy name, O most High'' (Ps. 92:1).

"Whoso offereth praise glorifieth me: and to him that ordereth his conversation aright will I shew the salvation of God'' (Ps. 50:23).

"Rejoice in the Lord, O ye righteous, for praise is comely for the upright'' (Ps.33:1).

I know of no better way to learn to praise the Lord than through praise passages in the Bible. The Psalms are full of praise, many of them given fully to prayers of praise. Read through the Psalms during the next thirty days and shade with a colored pencil those verses which pertain to praise. Then you will have a ready reference in praise. Sometimes, you can change a psalm *about* God to a psalm *to* God directly; for example, Psalm 23, "You are my shepherd, Lord, I shall not want. You make me to lie down in green pastures; you lead me beside the still waters. You restore my soul. You lead in the paths of righteousness for your name's sake. Yea, though I walk through the valley of the shadow of death, I will fear no evil: for thou are with me; thy rod and thy staff they comfort me. You prepare a table before me in the presence of my enemies; you anoint my head with oil; my cup runs over. Surely goodness and mercy shall follow me all the days of my life: and I will dwell in your house, O Lord forever."

The major portion of Psalm 119 is a pouring out of praise to God and declaration of response to God's Word. All except about a half-dozen of those 176 verses of prayer have references to God's Word in some form such as law, testimonies, precepts, statutes, word, judgments, commandments, and ordinances. You will find it a delight to make this prayer your own special personal prayer.

I have said previously that I make a habit of reading the entire book of Psalms through each month. Memorization is almost inevitable as you repeat such a project. Nothing has enhanced my praise life like the learning of the Psalms.

In the 2959 Prayer Plan that I have recommended there are whole pages given to nothing but praise. Each divider marking the special days of prayer is filled front and back with praises. After using the Bible in praises one will become accustomed to praise and will find it natural to praise the Lord with a Psalm or with words born in a praise-filled heart.

There are other segments of Scripture that form terrific texts of praise.

Most all of Exodus 15 is a song of praise unparalleled anywhere as far as I am concerned. It begins with, "I will sing unto the Lord, for he hath triumphed gloriously: the horse and his rider hath he thrown into the sea." The song of praise ends with, "Sing ye to the Lord, for he hath triumphed gloriously; the horse and his rider hath he thrown into the sea" (vv. 1,21).

The entirety of 2 Samuel 22 is a glorious song of praise on the occasion of David's deliverance. Here are some of the high peaks of the range of praise:

"The Lord is my rock, and my fortress, and my deliverer; The God of my rock . . . he is my shield, and the horn of my salvation, my high tower, and my refuge, my savior, thou savest me from violence. I will call on the Lord, who is worthy to be praised: so shall I be saved from mine enemies" (vv.2–4).

"For who is God, save the Lord? And who is a rock, save our God? God is my strength and power: and he maketh my way perfect. He maketh my feet like hinds' feet: and setteth me upon my high places" (vv.32–34).

"The Lord liveth; and blessed be my rock; and exalted be the God of the rock of my salvation. Therefore I will give thanks unto thee, O Lord, among the heathen, and I will sing praises unto thy name" (vv. 47,50).

May I suggest that one day soon you simply begin your time of prayer by reading slowly and aloud one of these great passages of praise?

When Solomon dedicated the Temple he said, "Blessed be the Lord God of Israel, which spake with his mouth into David my father, and hath with his hand fulfilled it. And the Lord hath performed his word that he spake. Lord, God of Israel, there is no God like thee, in heaven above, or on earth beneath, who keepest covenant and mercy with his servants that walk before thee with all their heart" (1 Kings 8:15,20,23). These were words of praise at the occasion of the dedication of the Temple when the glory of the Lord came and filled the Temple. When Solomon has finished this prayer of petition and praise, he stood before the altar and blessed the Lord. That prayer is recorded in 1 Kings, chapter 8.

Prior to that when David, Solomon's father was preparing the offering to build the Temple he said, "Blessed be thou, Lord God of Israel our father, for ever and ever. Thine, O, Lord, is the greatness, and the power, and the glory, and the victory, and majesty: for all that is in the heaven and the earth is thine; thine is the kingdom, O Lord, and thou art exalted as head above all. Both riches and honour come of thee, and thou reignest over all; and in thine hand is power and might; and in thine hand it is to make great, and to give strength unto all. Now therefore, our God, we thank thee, and praise thy glorious name. But who am I, and what is my people, that we should be able to offer so willingly after this sort? for all things come to thee, and of thine own have we given thee'' (1 Chron. 29:10–14). How wonderful it would be if a congregation broke into such a praise during the offertory one Sunday morning!

Thus you can see that the Bible is literally a library of resources in the practice of prayer. It is your *prayer book*. Get better acquainted with it. Ask God to quicken your love for it and to enliven you according to his Word.

---

1. E. M. Bounds, *Necessity of Prayer* (Grand Rapids: Baker Book House, 1976), p. 112.

Part 3
Seven Special Secrets of Prayer

The final pages of this book have to do with secrets in prayer. I have discovered the following simple secrets to be of great worth in the prayer life. These chapters are brief and should be read and reread until the main thrust of truth comes through.

14

The Secret of Getting into Prayer

Prayer has a gate. We can best enter prayer by means of the gate. That gate is THANKSGIVING. Prayer has a court, a porch. That court is PRAISE. We are to "Enter into his gates with thanksgiving and into his courts with praise." We do this by means of the will (J.R.T.).

Make a joyful noise unto the Lord, all ye lands. Serve the Lord with gladness﹒ come before his presence with singing. Know ye that the Lord he is God: it is he that hath made us, and not we ourselves; we are his people, and the sheep of his pasture. Enter into his gates with thanksgiving, and into his courts with praise: be thankful unto him, and bless his name"(Ps. 100:1 4).

It is a general principle in the spiritual realm that problems yield great treasures of truth. Just as miracles generally begin with crises so spiritual secrets have their beginning in spiritual enigmas.

One of the great problems in prayer experienced by believers is the problem of varying emotions. If I prayed only when I felt like it, I would pray very little. I remember a message preached by Dr. Sidlow Baxter in which he shared a testimony of the evolution of his own prayer life in the quiet time. He decided that the early hour of the morning belonged to God and determined to get up and have that time alone with God. He declared that for the first several days he got up but his emotions refused to come to the place of prayer with him. He prayed without emotions but he continued to get up and meet God in the place of prayer. After several days, one morning he was praying and emotions decided to join him! He had a glorious good time in prayer. Now in this brief testimony is a valid principle. Man, in the area of his soul, is possessed with three great capacities. The first is his capacity to *know*, to reason, to think, his *intellectual* capacity. The second is his capacity to *feel*, his *emotional* capacity. The third is his capacity to *decide*, his *will* or *volitional* capacity.

The success of anyone in the prayer life will be determined by the order of authority of these capacities! I want you to remember this!

If the *emotions* reign, the prayer life will greatly suffer. If we wait for the good time, the high feelings, the great emotional moments, we will grow discouraged. The emotions are ever influenced by too many things which are continuously changing. Emotions are affected by the amount of sleep, the digestive processes, the functioning of the vital inner organs such as the liver. (It has been set forth that the liver is probably more influential over one's actual emotions than any other organ of the body!) Wind, heat, cold, barometric pressure, or clouds can affect and influence the emotions. Emotions are not wrong, but it is wrong to allow the emotions to reign in the life. The result of emotions reigning will be continuing variations and helpless inconsistencies.

If the *intellect* reigns, the result will be much the same as when emotions reign. Human intellect is at the mercy of its own observations. It has two great problems. The first is that it does not have the final report of all the facts on any given subject. The second is that the facts it does have are colored by its own interpretations and its biased point of view. Prayer can neither be established nor maintained on emotions or intellect.

The *will* is the nearest quality in man to sovereignty because it links man, when properly exercised, to the sovereignty of God. All animals and life, higher forms as well as lower, seem to obey certain predesigned rules and operate according to an instinctual pattern. The higher forms of life have *intellect* in the sense that memory patterns can be stored and responses altered and fixed. Many of them seem to have emotional capacities and be capable of showing joy or sadness. Only man has "free" will and is accountable for his choices and actions. This means that he can not only choose to soar above the animal world in an existence blessed by his God but he can sink beneath the animal level in a sin-cursed existence without God. Now, I have said all this to suggest that as we come to prayer, the *will* should be foremost in our capacities in getting into and the continuing adventure of prayer.

The Will to Pray

The will is the key! Unlike *emotions*, it has the capacity to act independently of feelings. Unlike the *mind*, it has the capacity to act independently of thinking. In that sense the *will* is sovereign. The *will* has the power to do something with which *emotions* may not concur or the *mind* understand. We must *will* to pray because the Word of God has both invited and commanded us to pray. I am not equipped *emotionally* to *feel* all that prayer can mean or all that it is. I am not equipped *mentally* to *understand* all that prayer is. Therefore, with a decision of the *will* I choose to engage in an endeavor I can not fathom emotionally or intellectually. *I must learn to live then in the realm of the will!* I have found no fact in recent days which has helped me more in every area of the Christian walk than this one fact.

When I will to respond to the will of God as set forth in the Word of God, God's power is released to perform that which he has willed in me. God wants me to pray. He has commanded me to pray. With my will I can choose to pray and my will throws God's will into gear and I pray in his power!

The Will to Praise

The first crisis in prayer is found in the early moments of prayer. Prayer is not easy. The enemy sees to that! Anything at a premium comes with great effort and cost. *I have discovered that prayer has a gate and a front porch!* Look back to the Scripture at the beginning of this chapter. "Enter into his gates with thanksgiving, and into his courts with praise." Now here is a vital secret of prayer. I have been commanded to approach God with thanksgiving and praise. I am to enter the *gate* with thanksgiving and stand in the *court* with *praise*. Even if I don't feel emotionally grateful or have intellectual understanding of the matter of praise, I can choose with an act of my will to give thanks and praise. We are not commanded to *feel* grateful; that is an emotion. We are commanded to *give thanks;* that is an act of the will.

The psalmist becomes our example here. "I will bless the Lord at all times: his praise shall continually be in my mouth. My soul shall make her boast in the Lord: the humble shall hear thereof and be glad. O magnify the Lord with me and let us exalt his name together" (Ps. 34:1–3). He is acting out of his *will*. Again he says, "I will offer unto thee the sacrifice of thanksgiving, and will call upon the name of the Lord. I will pay my vows unto the Lord now in the presence of all his people, In the courts of the Lord's house, in the midst of thee, O Jerusalem. Praise ye the Lord" (Ps. 116:17–19). Notice in these passages the dominance of the *will*.

There is a verse found in three places in the Psalms which is identical except for a few words. "Why are thou cast down, O my soul? And why art thou disquieted within me? hope thou in God: for I shall yet praise him, . . . who is the health of my countenance, and my God" (Ps. 42:5, 11; Ps. 43:5). It seems to me that here the psalmist is having difficulty with his emotions (his soul). He is cast down and disquieted. But he chooses to take command of his emotions by the means of his will. In effect he is saying, "Soul, you are incorrect in your assessments of the situations. I command you to bless the Lord and find your hope in him! He is your health, your help, and your hope!"

Again in Psalm 103 the psalmist is taking command of his soul saying, "Bless the Lord, O my soul, and all that is within me" (v. 1). Now this is extremely important in the prayer life. Leave not your prayer time at the mercy of your emotions or understanding. Set your will to pray regularly and continuously. When it is hardest to pray, choose to pray the hardest!

The Set of the Will

Determine that you will pray because it is right. Vow to stand with your will in cooperation with the will of God. Only when we will to pray can the Holy Spirit make the most by helping our infirmities. His "help" is conditioned on our willingness to take up the matter of prayer on our part.

I have found that the will can be set like an alarm clock. If I go to bed at night with a set of the will to get up regardless of how I feel, God seems to honor that and gives his great aid.

As you choose to get into prayer via thanksgiving and praise, allow your ears to hear your vocal declaration, "I will to give thanks and to praise the Lord! I will to continue to pray whether I *feel* or not, whether I *understand* or not!"

The will to give thanks and praise is a vital secret in prayer.

15

The Secret of Praying Always

No man will pray always who neglects the formation of the habit of regular prayer. The disciple who regularly observes a place and time and method will gradually find the habit learned in the secret place is binding through all the public life. A confirmed habit of regular prayer will create regularity and constancy amidst all irregularities of time and place and method. Prayer in the secret place will create a spirit which will obtain in all public places. FELLOWSHIP WITH GOD AS AN ACTIVITY WILL ISSUE IN FELLOWSHIP WITH GOD AS AN ATTITUDE (G. Campbell Morgan).[1]

And he spake a parable unto them to this end, that men ought always to pray, and not faint (Luke 18:1).
Pray without ceasing (1 Thess. 5:17).
Praying always with all prayer and supplication in the Spirit (Eph. 6:18).

Each of these Scriptures bear out one common implication, namely, that man should always be praying. If we view this command from the human side we will shrink back and exclaim, "It cannot be done! It is impossible!" And humanly it is impossible. But it is upon human impossibilities that divine possibilities are foundationed! We could simply rationalize and dilute the commands to mean that we should pray *regularly* not *continuously*. But to do so would be to rob prayer of one of its most vital aspects.

The Prayer Cycle

Prayer is a cycle which began with God. Prayer is *from* the Father, *in* the Son, *through* the Spirit, *to* the Father. In this sense there is a fellowship of prayer going on within the trinity—the Father, the Son, and the Spirit! When I come to prayer, I am simply getting in on what has been going on continuously.

If I am commanded to pray always and without ceasing, there is inherent within the command the promise of my being able to do so.

What the Command Does Not Mean

The protest of our reason is that we cannot pray always because there are other things to be done. The reason is correct in that it is impossible to spend twenty-four hours of every day engaged physically, mentally, and spiritually in the endeavor of prayer. This is obviously not what Jesus or Paul was suggesting.

Ejaculatory Prayer

G. Campbell Morgan in his book, *The Practice of Prayer*, suggests that our fathers used to speak of and practice ejaculatory prayer. This is prayer in the sudden, immediate sense and suggests the ability to pray the right prayer without a moment's notice. It has the suggestion of "praying in the nick of time." It is folly to imagine that in a great crowd of folks when a need arises externally or internally, prayer must wait for the right time and chosen place.

Ejaculatory prayer suggests that flowing just beneath the surface of the conscious life prayer is taking place as an attitude and spirit. And when there is a demand of any sort prayer comes to the surface immediately and expresses desires in accord with the will of God. Morgan says, "It would be a great gain to all of us if we could learn again the method and practice it." [2]

The Secret

The command to pray always undoubtedly suggests the possibility of continuing in the atmosphere and attitude of prayer. Such an attitude will mean that in immediate crises *prayer* not *panic* will result! But how can I remain in such an attitude of prayer so as to guarantee such a wonderful prospect. Here is the secret: The *attitude* of prayer is guaged by the *act* of prayer. The activity of prayer will eventuate in an *attitude* of prayer. The *atmosphere* of prayer will never be any greater than is the measure and worth of *activity* of prayer. I have found that if the day *begins* with the right *activity* of prayer, it is apt to continue in the right *attitude* of prayer.

I am finding that when my habit of daily prayer is more nearly what it should be, my spur-of-the moment praying is more likely to be "on target."

A perfect example of this secret is found in the case of King Jehoshaphat of Judah. In 2 Chronicles 17 we read that "The Lord was with Jehoshaphat, because he walked in the first ways of his father David, and sought not unto Baalim; but sought to the Lord God of his father, and walked in his commandments, and not after the doings of Israel" (vv. 3–4). The result was that the Lord established the kingdom in his hand . . . and his heart was lifted up in the ways of the Lord" (2 Chron. 17:5–6). Doubtlessly Jehoshaphat was a man of regular prayer habits. The record declares that he was a man who sought the Lord. In 2 Chronicles 20 there is a great crisis in which the Moabites and the Ammonites mounted a great invasion. When the news reached Jehoshaphat, instead of responding with *panic* as he might reasonably have done, he responded with *prayer*. "And Jehoshaphat feared, and set himself to seek the Lord" (2 Chron. 20:3). The next verses are occupied with one of the greatest prayers ever recorded. Take time to read it. The prayer ended like this, "O our God, wilt thou not judge them? for we have no might against this great company that cometh against us; neither know we what to do: but our eyes are up on thee" (2 Chron. 20:12). The immediate response of God through his prophet was, "Be not afraid nor dismayed by reason of this great multitude; for the battle is not yours, but God's" (2 Chron. 20:15). Jehoshaphat knew the value of ejaculatory prayer—the spur-of-the-moment prayer. But here is the whole point: Jehosaphat sought the Lord in the emergency because his regular habit was to seek thee Lord in the quiet place. His *attitude* of prayer in the moment of desperation was flavored by his *activity* of prayer in the quiet place.

You know, of course, the result. The people of Judah stood up to praise the Lord and went out to meet the enemy army singing,

"Praise the Lord; for his mercy endures forever." As they did, God set the armies of the enemy in confusion against each other and they were utterly destroyed with no need of Jehoshaphat's army to fight. The end result is described in 2 Chronicles 20:25, "And when Jehoshaphat and his people came to take away the spoil of them, they found among them in abundance both riches with the dead bodies, and precious jewels, which they stripped off for themselves, more than they could carry away: and they were three days in gathering of the spoil, it was so much." Their problems through praise had become their prosperity!

The act of prayer in the quiet place will bring about the *attitude* of prayer in *praying always*.

---

1. G. Campbell Morgan, *The Practice of Prayer* (Alexandria, La.: Lamplighter Publications, nd), p. 112.

2. *Ibid.*, p. 113.

16

The Secret of Transactional Prayer

There is a kind of prayer that we need to learn. It involves a definite transaction with God. Generalities are avoided. Time is saved and results are obtained. It is common-sense kind of prayer. This is a wonderful way of faith. To commit everything to God and bow before him in prayer till we believe him; and then stand upon our standing of faith, praising him. Every moment of faith is a moment of God's working, whether we see it or not; his Word is true, God answers prayer, and there is no kind of prayer that is more effective than the prayer of committal (John Lindsay in tract entitled "The Prayer of Committal").

Commit thy way unto the Lord; trust also in him; and he shall bring it to pass (Ps. 37:5).

And this is the confidence that we have in him, that if we ask any thing according to his will, he heareth us: And if we know that he hear us, whatsoever we ask, we know that we have the petitions that we desired of him (1 John 5:14–15).

I begin this important chapter with a light warning. I use the qualifying word "light" because I do not want to frighten the reader out of employing one of the most effective kinds of praying there is. On the other hand I want to encourage discretion in how to pray at varying times.

A professional golfer stands in the fairway 275 yards away from the green. His caddy stands beside the golf cart a few feet away.

There are different clubs for different purposes. Being a professional, the golfer intuitively knows which club will do the job he desires
to be done. Thus, he makes his selection. Likewise, the prevailing
pray-er on the basis of divine revelation, years of experience, and
knowledge of the situation knows just what kind of prayer to pray.
His knowledge of the kind of prayer to employ and how to pray is a
vital secret in the prayer life.

While it is generally agreed that there are five basic kinds or forms
of prayer, it is also the concensus among many that there are other
stages in prayer worth discussing. The five accepted forms of prayer
are:

Confession, thanksgiving, petition, intercession, and praise. We
have already discussed such as *rehearsing spiritual truth* and *putting
on the spiritual armor.* Other forms of prayer may be *the spoken
word of faith* or various forms of *standing in prayer to resist the
enemy.* These and others may not be so much forms in themselves as
they are *stages* of prayer.

I have found nothing more helpful than the realization that the
Holy Spirit stands to help me in prayer, which means that I can know
how and what to pray in any given instance, if I wait on the Lord.
One situation may need *prevailing intercession* while another may
need *resistance of the enemy.* Still another may call simply for *praise
and thanksgiving in faith.* A clear example is noted in the experience
of Joshua. Joshua said, "Shout; for the Lord hath given you the city"
(Josh. 6:16). Now, at this point it would have been foolish for Joshua
and the people to begin to pray like this, "Lord, we pray that you
give us this city!" It was not the time to *petition;* it was time to
praise with a shout of faith!

We come now to a kind of prayer that is all too rare among
believers today. I agree that it may be more a stage of prayer than
another form of prayer. I call it *transactional prayer.*

The two passages of Scripture at the beginning of this chapter
sound rather transactional. That is, they suggest that we can pray
knowingly, transact business, and be on with it. *There is a time for
such a manner of prayer.*

"Stake-driving" Prayer

The story is told of a farmer who had great problems of inconsis-

tency and instability in his Christian life. He would consecrate
himself to the Lord and later fall into doubting and temptation. The
devil seemed to torment him continuously. One day the farmer was
moved to make a transaction with God. He would give himself to the
Lord once-and-for all. To symbolize the place and the reality of his
commitment, he decided to literally drive down a stake in the ground
at the definite place where it happened. Upon a day not far removed,
the devil attacked and began his line of accusation. Whereupon the
farmer simply replied, "Come this way, Mr. Devil, here is the spot
where I gave myself to God, and this is the stake I drove, and this is
the place where God accepted me." This definiteness lifted him up
above all doubts and suggestions of the enemy.

Prayer that Destroys Faith

In contrast to transactional prayer is a kind of prayer that prays one
out of faith. While there is a time to plead and prevail, asking God
for a definite answer, it would be a mistake to pray in such a manner
if the answer was already in our hearts. It is vain to keep on asking
for something when we know that it is God's will to give it. This is
the time to *receive* it instead of request it. We first receive it in our
hearts and then in our *hands*. If one of my children asked for
something, knowing that it was my intention to give it, and continued to ask as if they had never asked before, I would be insulted. I
would believe that he or she distrusted my integrity. Whereas, if my
son or daughter asked for something, believing that I was intending
to give it and began thanking me for it, I would be pleased. I would
even be pleased if there was a reminder every now and then. We are
invited by the Lord to "Put me in remembrance" (Isa. 43:26).

Examples of Transactional Prayer

A praying woman pleaded continuously for the salvation of her
rebellious son. One day at prayer she had the sudden impression that
it was time to stop pleading and start thanking God and confessing
the salvation of her son to be a reality. She thus received the
salvation of her son in her heart. She even confessed it openly that he
would be saved. She was more audacious than that! She asserted his
salvation in the present tense. She told other intercessors, "You can
stop praying for my son's salvation. He is saved as of now!" As a

matter of visible fact, the lad was not saved. But the mother knew something by faith. She knew that "Faith was an act and an affirmation of the act that bids eternal truth be present fact." The son was informed of his mother's declaration and went on in his sinful ways. But within a matter of days, almost without visible aid, he was gloriously converted and instantaneously changed. When he announced the news of his conversion to his mother with great excitement and joy, her response was, "I've been trying to tell you this for three weeks!" She had experienced the joy of *transactional prayer*.

George Müller was a great man of prayer. It might be better said that he was a man of *great prayer*. He prayed in millions of dollars in provisions without ever letting his needs be made known to another human being.

One of the most beautiful stories involved the simple prayer of a child. The little girl, whose name was Abigail, had wanted for some time a multicolored woolen ball. One day Mr. Müller came to her home to visit her parents. Hearing that he was a man of prayer, she asked him if he would join her in prayer for the gift she desired. He answered that he would pray for her but that she also must pray.

The two knelt down together. She prayed first, asking God for the multicolored woolen ball. Then the man of God put his hand on her and prayed this prayer: *Father, here is a child who wishes to have a woolen ball in many colors. Nobody knows about this, and I too will not do anything about it. This is your business. Please hear her prayer.* Upon ending the prayer, he waited for a few seconds as if he was still praying. Then he got up and told the child that she would have her many-colored woolen ball in two days. Her heart leaped for joy! She wondered who would bring the ball to her but she never doubted that it would come. The second night after her prayer, in came her father from his store with just the kind of ball she had mentioned in her prayer. The next day Mr. Müller saw the little girl. He did not ask her if she had received the ball. He asked her if she found her new ball most interesting! He knew the Lord and together they experienced *transactional prayer*.

In the midst of this writing, as is often the case, there was such an experience of transactional prayer that I am compelled to share it.

A friend called who had come to recognize that there was a continued and repeated problem in his life that had been the source of

much conflict and heartache as well as deprivation. On the basis of
the Word of God, and our convictions constructed thereon, we went
to prayer one afternoon. I do not always rely on sensations, impres-
sions, and feelings but there are times when their presence cannot be
denied, and *need* not be denied.

We had a great time of prayer. There was a sense of peace and
relief when we had finished as if we had made a certain transaction
. . . and indeed we had. The victory was won! There was no doubt!
We are standing now in the joy and certainty of that victory. Each
confirmation is simply an "amen" to an already certain transaction
and not reassurances to a sagging faith. From God's view (and thus
ours) it is counted done! We stand on that. This is transactional
prayer.

You will find many cases of this kind of prayer in the Bible. It will
prove an interesting endeavor for you to go through the Bible and
find those situations where such prayer was the order of the day.
Here are just a few:

Elijah on Mount Carmel had a positive and definite transaction
with God. He prayed a prayer of less than one hundred words and the
fire came down out of heaven and consumed the sacrifice. His whole
life was instance after instance of transactional prayer.

Elisha had learned from Elijah, and Elijah's God was his God as
well! A while after Elijah's departure into heaven Elisha encountered
a crisis. A whole enemy army was sent to Dothan to capture him.
The army surrounded the city. The excited servant of Elisha reported
the hopelessness of the situation to him. Then Elisha prayed, "Lord,
open his eyes, that he may see." That was all he prayed. "And the
Lord opened the eyes of the young man; and he saw: and, behold, the
mountain was full of horses and chariots of fire round about Elisha"
(2 Kings 6:17). They had an immediate transaction!

We have already referred to Jehoshaphat and his prayer in 2
Chronicles 20 as an example of the accord between the activity of
prayer and the attitude of prayer. He is also an ideal example of
transactional prayer as he presents the cause to the Lord by saying,
"We know not what to do. Our eyes are on you." He had prayed the
prayer of committal and counted it done. When this happened, God
went into action.

A casual investigation of the miracles of Jesus will reveal that they were cases of transactional prayer or prayers of committal in which the problem was exposed to the Father, committed to him, and left for the accomplishment of his perfect will.

I suggest that the reader begin to observe the possibility that there might be such a situation presently in existence that calls for transactional prayer. There is no better time for you to find out that it works than right now!

You know the will of God, now drive your stake. Stand on God's standing and count it done! Refuse the latest news of your senses. Reject the common concensus. Sign the contract. Believe it done as of now! Stand on that! You have it in your heart now! It will be in your hand later!

"Give it to the Lord! Trust in him and he will do the work!" That is a rough paraphrase of Psalm 37:5. If you are asking something in God's will, then you know that he has heard! If he has heard, then you have! How do you know? He said so! (1 John 5:14–15). Try transactional prayer today.

17

The Secret of Praying
from the Ground of Redemption

In intercession you bring the person, or the circumstance that impinges on you before God until you are moved by His attitude towards that person or circumstance. . . . When we pray on the ground of Redemption, God creates something He can create in no other way than through intercessory prayer (Oswald Chambers).[1]

The vantage point of prayer is all-important. I have picked up a term mentioned in passing by Oswald Chamber in *My Utmost for His Highest* and spent considerable time with its implications. The term is a part of the title for this chapter, "Praying from the Ground of Redemption."

While prayer in one sense is a cycle, it is in another sense a triangle. That triangle has God at one point, the object or problem at another point, and the one praying at the final point. We pray from one of those vantage points. If we pray from the ground of the problem as we see it, we will be *problem* conscious. If we pray from the ground of ourselves, we will be *self-conscious*. If we pray from the ground of who God is and what he has done, we will be God-conscious. *Problem-consciousness* will yield mourning and despair. *Self-consciousness* will produce guilt and morbid introspection. *God-consciousness* will bring gladness and purpose as well as victory. Praying from God's vantage point is what I call praying from the ground of redemption.

The Alternative to Praying from the Ground of Redemption

Before we look at what it means to pray from the ground of

redemption, let us see the sad alternatives. We have already glanced at them. Proper prayer begins with God. Improper prayer begins with the problem. Now, make no mistake, we pray from within the problem many times but our vantage point is God's point of view, not ours. Let us take a hypothetical example. I am called upon to pray for a backslidden believer. I say backslidden because I am satisfyingly certain that he has been genuinely born again. If I pray from the standpoint of what my eyes see and hear, I will pray from the viewpoint of disappointment. The prognosis is poor for recovery from every human standpoint. I pray, but the praying is pressed by what my eyes have seen. It is mighty distressing. I pray, but my soul is quashed by the prevailing knowledge of how bad the problem is. I get off the ground in my praying but the law of visible conditions pulls like the relentless law of gravity and my prayers "crash and burn." I pray, but my prayers are plaintive, pleading, mournful, and, at the best, only hopeful! When I am through there is more despair than delight. I have prayed from the ground of circumstances as I see them, situations as I judge them, and possibilities as I view them. Visibility from here is zero, partly cloudy, and there's a chance for showers. I have prayed from the problem instead of from God!

I greatly fear that most of our crisis praying is on this tragic basis. We plead, we hope, we mourn but our souls are weighted down too heavy for "soaring prayer."

If we pray from self-consciousness, the result will be worse yet. We will never pray! The enemy gets us past the point of confession and begins to accuse us, "You are not worthy to pray! You don't belong here in the court of God! Look at your record! You are a flunk out! God has no reason to answer your prayers!" And you know, he is essentially right.

You may reply if you desire, "You know, Satan, you are right about me. I am worthless by myself. I have no right here at God's throne by myself. I am a flunk out by myself. God has no reason to answer my prayers by myself. But you remember I am not by myself. I am in Jesus and he is in me, . . . we are one! I am here in his name because of his worthiness, his purity, his record, his standing in the court of God. Now if you will pardon me, I have business to do. Get out of my way!"

The only alternatives to praying on the ground of redemption are these two: praying from the ground of the problem and from the ground of self. One produces *gloom* and *despair*, and other produces *guilt* and *defeat*.

What Is This Kind of Prayer?

We have rejected the feasibility of praying from either of the other two points of the triangle of prayer. Now, let us investigate what it means to pray from the point where God is. If I stand where I am and where the problem is, I have only that information that can be known in my mind and that has accrued up to now. I neither have all the facts nor the sense to properly interpret the facts that I have. When I stand on ground with God, I have all the truth in the Word—past, present, and future.

Now, let us suppose that I am praying for that same backslider that I mentioned in a previous paragraph. I am not standing on new ground, God and his redemptive plan. I look for the moment at the problem (the backslider), for another moment at the one who prays (myself) to be sure that all is well in my relationship, but I firmly fix my sight on God, truth, the ultimate revelation of God. I soon discover new heart to my praying. I find that God is able to perform what he began. I am reminded that we (including the backslider) are God's workmanship created in Christ Jesus unto good works, fore-ordained to walk in them. I find that the one for whom I am praying is to be conformed to the image of God's Son. I see reality from the finished work of redemption and pray with authority for that one who is *not* the devil's property but God's. I pray in faith, counting those things I have not seen as though they were. My spirit is lifted into fellowship with the Father and his plans. I agree with God and what he has said about this person. I have prayed and my soul has taken wings! I can see from a new point of view.

I am praying at this moment for a very dear loved one who has a broken heart. Last night she wept and sobbed and sobbed and wept until the only thing I could do was weep with her. I went to my room to pray for her with great inward pain. I asked the Father how he wanted me to pray. I saw it! If I chose to pray from the ground of conditions as I saw them, I would weep with her in hopelessness. More prayer would mean more despair. *I must pray for her from the ground of redemption.* She is God's child! He loves her! Christ has died for her and lives in her. He prayed for her and still prays for her. One of the prayers that he has prayed for her is that his joy might be fulfilled in her. *God will answer that prayer!* The psalmist said, "Weeping endures for the night but joy comes in the morning." From this ground I can even thank God for the heartache and heartbreak. Character is being developed. Integrity is being strengthened. Enlargement through distress is coming to pass. Again from this point of view I remember that the psalmist said, "It is good for me that I have been afflicted; that I might learn thy statutes. I know . . . that thou in faithfulness have afflicted me. This is my comfort in my affliction: for thy word hath quickened me"(Ps. 119:50,71,75).

After praying in this manner and at this level, my heart, still heavy in human sympathy, has soared to the heavenlies. I have prayed from the ground of redemption!

Praying from the ground of redemption gives us heaven's point of view and we can then pray with authority toward changes in the situations of earth. We pray from the fresh point of view of the will of God.

I will no longer pray from the natural point of view where the sadness of conditions is compounded by the fact that I cannot cope with them on a human level. I will pray from heaven's side, agreeing that anything God has said, I have a right to believe and repeat. No longer will my mind be weighted down with the dark assessment of the situation gathered along the lines of what eyes have seen and ears have heard. I will not pray on the basis of *what he has seen and what he has said!* Praise the Lord!

Here is the key to praying from the ground of redemption. I will *glance* at the problem and I will *gaze* at God! From henceforth the problem will have the *glance* and God will have my *gaze!* I will gaze at God until I know him in such a manner that the problem will have no significance but as a pointer to God's great resources! From here it's a clear day and you can see forever!

---

1. Chambers., *op. cit.*, p. 348.

18

The Secret of Praying Down Stronghoulds

We need to be constantly reminded that prayer is to God, for man, and against the devil. We must know that any prayer to God is against Satan. This "against" factor must not be forgotten or else we will have war without an enemy. In Ephesians 6 the key word in the engagement which we face is "against." "Stand against the wiles of the devil, not against flesh and blood, but against principalities, against powers, against the rulers of the darkness of this world; against spiritual wickedness in high places." In prayer the entrenchments of the enemy must be a primary target! (Author Unknown).

The weapons of our warfare are not carnal, but mighty through God to the pulling down of strongholds; Casting down imaginations, and every high thing that exalteth itself against the knowledge of God, and bringing into captivity every thought to the obedience of Christ; And having in a readiness to revenge all disobedience, when your obedience is fulfilled (2 Cor. 10:4-6).

We have seen that prayer is *worship, work,* and *warfare.* There is a sense in which all prayer has qualities of all three but in a special sense there are stages of forms of prayer that are particularly effective in a given area. For instance *praise* and *thanksgiving* particularly enhance *worship; intercession* and *petition* implement *work* toward man; while, the *word of faith, rehearsing the truth,* and *resistance in*

144

prayer are directed toward the devil.

Most of the Christian world seems to have taken a vow of silence on the subject of the devil and spiritual warfare. There is nothing in the Bible to support either the silence regarding the devil or present-day teaching that God's children should ignore him and his activities. This silence and disregard has but given him more operating room unmolested. There are few discoveries within the framework of the Christian life that will provide new impetus and victory as the discovery of our authority in the name of Jesus over the devil and how to exercise it. Vital praying demands that we recognize that the devil is our "adversary" (1 Pet. 5:8–9).

I come to discuss something that is to me a vital secret in prayer, *Praying down strongholds*. For more than a dozen years it has been a vital form of praying with me that accomplishes something that is accomplished in no other form of praying.

We shall deal with the subject under three headings: One, *defining* strongholds; two, *detecting* strongholds; and three, *demolishing* strongholds.

Defining Strongholds

The word for stronghold in the Greek is a military word which is synonymous with "fortress." It is taken from a verb of the same root which means "to make firm." In military language it would refer to an area where the enemy is entrenched. In spiritual terms it is precisely the same, a place where the enemy is entrenched.

I am now convinced after many years of counseling the troubled, that many of those with whom we deal have something closely akin to or identifiable as a stronghold.

A stronghold may be an area of thought, a fixation in the mind, a complex which occupies a vital area of thinking. It may be something that is largely subconscious, like an iceberg, with only a small portion above the surface.

Modern psychology seems to have been moderately effective in probing back into one's past to discover the causes of many present problems. It is in the treatment of such that the success has been less than satisfying. The fallacy of much of the field of modern psychology is that of supposing that man is only body and soul and treating him on this basis. The devil operates largely in the area of the soul, concentrating on the mind. He is quite willing to take advantage of any encouragement we give him whether it is willingly or ignorantly given. Our aversion, for the greater part, to openly discuss and openly confront the devil is a source of his greatest encouragement.

A stronghold may be partly or wholly physical. This is not to say that it is unreal as a physical malady and is purely a matter of the imagination. However, there are physical symptoms which will disappear when a spiritual or mental problem is solved. It is an undeniable conclusion among both religious and secular specialists that much of our physical illness would be healed with the healing of the soul and spirit.

The existence of a problem does not mean that one has a stronghold. For instance, the existence of worry does not mean that a person has a stronghold of worry. The probability is good, however, that if one gives in to worrying much and often, there will soon be a stronghold in which that person is bound and the matter of worry is no longer voluntary but compulsive.

The verses in 2 Corinthians 10 surely refer to other strongholds in the spiritual atmosphere as well as those in the personal life. It is with the latter that we will deal here.

Now, in summary, let us define a stronghold as a system of thought or area of bondage within the mind or body which encourages the devil. As strange as it may seem, a stronghold can begin in the preconscious child. Attitudes of parents, especially the mother, may leave the child open for the establishing of strongholds in the life of the little one.

A full treatment of this subject could well be the subject of a whole volume. Thus it is not likely that we can make clear here all the reader's curiosity will call for. I suggest that you pray that God would use this brief chapter to set you off on a study of your own. Our thrust here has to do with *prayer* and strongholds.

Detecting Strongholds

Compulsions, obessions, fixations, and recurring involuntary thought processes would be included as suspects for strongholds. Unreasoning fear, helpless hate, unavoidable jealousy, violent temper, or a driving, aggressive spirit may be symptoms of a stronghold. Uncontrollable lust, unchecked appetites, or undeniable urges may be telltale signs. Incontinence (lack of self-restraint), impatience, or even indecision may be signs of a developing stronghold.

I have seen people with what I thought to be strongholds of rejection (a most common one), lust, timidity, distrust, criticism, and phobias of varying natures. At last count there were upwards of one hundred different phobias with the number increasing almost daily. I have seen folks with unreasoning fear of storms, high places, crowds, being alone, being with dead bodies, water, being photographed, and on and on, ad infinitum!

I have counseled with people who have tried everything to rid themselves of a terrible recurring fear or compulsion. No amount of encouragement or enlightenment regarding the nature of the problem seemed to help. But when the matter was diagnosed as a stronghold of a spiritual nature and dealt with on that basis, the healing was instantaneous. It is a healing as certain as is physical healing and in certain types of cases may include physical healing.

I have discussed this matter of strongholds with people from all walks of life and have been encouraged to intensify the study. I have spoken with hundreds of people, explaining to them the nature of a stronghold, to find them saying, "That's it! That is what has been wrong!" In a recent meeting it was obvious that the Lord was leading me to preach a message on strongholds. I had never done this in such a meeting before. It was a spiritual battle all day to study and a spiritual battle to preach that night. If feelings had reigned, I would not even have given an invitation. But as the invitation was given for folks to come to the Lord to have an area of their lives that was under bondage liberated, more than 70 percent of that congregation left their seats!

Demolishing Strongholds

Our weapons are mighty to the demolishing (pulling down) of strongholds. It is not specified in the Bible just what our weapons involve. We have been told to be strong in the Lord; to stand and having done all to stand; to withstand, which means to fling off; and to fight the good fight. We have also been reminded that our weapons are not carnal, that is, not of the flesh. We can safely assume that the Bible is chief among our weapons. I do not mean the physical book as much as I mean the system of truth that is contained therein. It is the truth in the Book, not the physical Book itself, which paralyzes the devil with fear. I remind you that in Ephesians 6:17 the sword of the Spirit is the *rhema* and not the *logos*. That is, the offensive weapon in the Christian's hand is that part of the Bible that has been enlived and personalized into revelation truth! For a fuller discussion of the difference between the *rhema* and the *logos* refer to the chapter, "The Word of God and Personal Prayer."

I am aware of the issue of the name and blood of Jesus in spiritual warfare. The use of the all-conquering name of Jesus seems to have great import in spiritual warfare. That name includes all that he is. His blood symbolizes all that he did in our behalf at Calvary and embraces the victory he won over the enemy. "And having spoiled principalities and powers, . . . triumphing over them in it"(Col. 2:15).

We get a hint in Revelation 12:11 as to how the enemy is overcome. "And they overcame him by the *blood* of the Lamb, and by the word of their testimony; and they loved not their lives unto the death." This indicates that the blood of Jesus, coupled with Christian testimony and total commitment, will mean the undoing of the devil.

Whatever you may wish to include in your arsenal of spiritual weaponry, the issue here is that prayer is the warfare, the engagement, the assault upon the stronghold that must be demolished.

When we come against an area in our lives or in that of someone else, we are coming in the name of Jesus, on the authority of the Word of God, standing in victory attained by the shedding of his blood. He that is within us, the Lord Jesus, is greater than the devil in the world. The declaration of the Word is that our weapons are mighty to the doing of four things:

The pulling down of strongholds.

The casting down of imaginations.

The putting down of high things.

The bringing into captivity of every thought to the obedience of Christ.

I believe that you will find that as you mobilize your spiritual arsenal with prayer, no stronghold can stand before the onslaught of our risen, conquering Lord! The removal of reasonings is as vital as the destruction of the stronghold. I frankly do not know what is involved in the "high things" mentioned in our passage. This could involve traditions, customs, cultures, or a myriad of other things. The good thing to know is that our weapons put them down! In the process of the mighty advance of our prayers, thoughts are taken captive! Imagine that! You and I through prayer can have effect on the thinking of those around us.

Begin with yourself. Identify a stronghold. Confess the sins that have aided that stronghold and perhaps caused it. Dismiss the enemy just as you have encouraged him before. Declare that you are God's property and he (the devil) is a trespasser. Confess that your body is the temple of the Holy Spirit who lives in you. Take your stand against any encroachment of the enemy in your mind and body. Declare your right to be free in Christ. Receive you freedom! Thank God for it. Then stand ready to help others in becoming whole people in Christ.

As you discover this secret, your prayer life will take on new meaning. As you come to the end of this chapter, I suggest that you memorize the passage with which we began (2 Cor. 10:4–6).

19

The Secret of Meditation in Prayer

Meditation has come of age! Millions are doing it. Introduced less than twenty years ago, transcendental meditation is sweeping our country like a contagion. More than 8,000 certified instructors are guiding adherents in the art of meditation in businesses, schools, institutions, and homes. More than 15,000 Americans monthly are attracted to the claims of TM! The Christian world has been silent long enough. This is another case of the devil taking a basic Christian art and perverting it to his own use. Meditation of the right sort is both validated and encouraged in the bible! Let us then know what needs to be known in this vital area of Christian awareness and growth (J. R. T.).

Blessed is the man who walketh not in the counsel of the ungodly, nor standeth in the way of sinners, nor sitteth in the seat of the scornful. BUT his delight is in the law of the LORD; and in his law doth he meditate day and night (Ps. 1:1–2).

This book of the law shall not depart out of thy mouth; but thou shalt meditate therein day and night, that thou mayest observe to do according to all that is written therein: for then thou shalt make thy way prosperous, and then thou shalt have good success (Josh. 1:8).

My soul shall be satisfied as with marrow and fatness; and my mouth shall praise thee with joyful lips: When I remember thee upon my bed, and meditate on thee in the night watches (Ps. 63:5–6). I remember the days of old; I meditate on all thy works; I muse on the work of thy hands (Ps. 143:5).

I will meditate in thy statutes. I will meditate in thy precepts. I will meditate in thy word (Ps. 119:48,78,148).

I was ministering a while ago in a large Southern city. I opened the Sunday paper to discover that in one of its supplements three full pages had been given to articles on transcendental meditation. The articles gave the history of TM and the phenomenal growth in the number of its adherents. The claim of TM is that with twenty minutes twice a day a life can be transformed. Maharishi Mahesh Yogi, a teacher in India, left his peaceful Himalayan retreat in 1958 to bring about what he called "the spiritual regeneration of the world."

I thought as I read those articles how wonderful it would be if Christians would be willing to engage themselves in prayer and meditation for a minimum of forty minutes a day. There would surely be a revival forthcoming.

Of the almost one hundred volumes I have read on prayer, only three give any measure of attention to meditation in any form! We have been shamefully silent on a vitally important form of prayer. Let us investigate it from a biblical view and come to a practical application of the principles involved.

The Meaning of Meditation

Meditation, in the proper sense, is not the throwing of the mind into neutral gear and accepting anything which comes. This is certain to open the door to the enemy who is waiting to take advantage of the slightest human encouragement.

In the biblical sense meditation has several implications. One word for meditate in the Old Testament means "to mutter" or "to muse." The picture here is that of subvocal review as if to whisper to ourselves. It has the quality of recounting and calling to remembrance. The passages listed at the first of this chapter use that word meaning "to mutter" (Ps. 1:2; Josh. 1:8; and Ps. 143:5). The passages in Psalm 119 use another Hebrew word which enriches the meaning of meditation. This word means to "bow down" in the sense of giving attention, respect, and worship.

In the New Testament the word for meditation is used sparingly. In fact there is only one instance of usage in the sense that we are using it. The word used means "to be careful," or "to take care of."

"Meditate upon these things; give thyself wholly to them; that thy profiting may appear to all" (1 Tim. 4:15). The other usage of that word is with the preposition to denote "before." Jesus had warned his people that they would be delivered up to synagogues and prisons, king and ruler. He said, "Settle it therefore in your hearts, not to meditate (to think about beforehand) before what we shall answer."

The Means of Meditation

There are certain principles which govern the matter of meditation. I will do little more than mention them as they are self-explanatory.

First, there is the principle of *isolation*. Hurry and crowds do not encourage meditation. It is not likely that there will be much meaningful meditation unless, and until, there is *isolation*.

Second, there is the principle of *concentration*. Attention is the act of the will. Concentration is sustained attention upon a specific object. The will can be disciplined and the power of concentration developed. Samuel Chadwick said, "Dreaming is not meditation. Dozing is not thinking. Moping is not praying. Prayer in the secret place demands every faculty at its best. Call every faculty of the mind and body to remembrance, recognition, and realization of the God that is in secret and seeth in secret. Hold the mind to this fact. Tolerate no distraction, allow no diversion, indulge no dissipation. Indispensable to profitable meditation is the matter of *concentration*.

Third, there is the principle of *memorization*. The psalmist declared, "Thy word have I hid in my heart" (119:11). To hide his Word in our hearts, we must commit it to memory. I believe that the level of *meditation* will never rise above the level of *memorization*. The Bible is to be the *text* of our meditation. It is God's *law* that we are to meditate day and night. No commentary will yield what God can reveal to the heart as the believer meditates on Scriptures committed to heart. As he mutters it, muses upon it, bows down before it, and gives careful attention to it, the deep meanings will spring forth. Good *memorization* leads to good *meditation!*

Fourth, there is the principle of *imagination*. What a wonderful gift is imagination. With it we can visit a mission field 10,000 miles away, soar to the heavenlies, and wash the feet of Jesus! That gift was meant to be used to the glory of God. It should be employed in the quiet place as we concentrate upon the Word of God.

Fifth, there is the principle of *repetition*. This is a valid principle in all learning procedures. In meditation we should repeat the Word until we have grasped it. An example of this principle came to me a moment ago. In Psalm 136 there are twenty-six verses, all of which contain the phrase "for his mercy endures for ever." Reading the Psalms every month every twenty-eighth day, I encounter this psalm. A while ago I simply asked the Lord, "Why the repetition!" As I read it again, the answer came. Here is a vital fact pertinent to everything we do and everything God does. Through repetition it had finally dawned on me, "his mercy really *is* forever!"

Sixth, there is the principle of *association*. Anything and everything can remind us of the Lord and our relationship with him through the principle of association.

The clouds can remind that he comes with clouds.

The rolling tides can remind us that his voice is mightier than the voice of many waters.

A clock can remind us of the timelessness of God and that there will soon come a point at which "time shall be no more."

A door, a light, a road, or a shepherd may remind us of our Lord Jesus Christ.

A flowing river serves to remind us that those who thirst, come, drink, and believe will have flowing from within rivers of living water!

With the Word of God as the background, every part of our world comes alive with the curriculum of meditation.

Put these words somewhere in your Bible or prayer notebook. Employ these principles when you come to the quiet place and begin to develop the art of meditation. Isolation, concentration, memorization, imagination, repetition, and association will prove to be profitable means of meditation.

Ministries of Meditation

What will be the result of meditation? Simply this, a man becomes what he thinks! "For as he thinketh in his heart, so is he" (Prov. 23:7). We become like what we think upon.

Meditation renews the mind, taking it from the harried, hurried world and riveting it to the eternal qualities of life.

Meditation restores calm to the soul. "Thou wilt keep him in perfect peace, whose mind is stayed on thee" (Isa. 26:3).

Meditation leads to stability of life. "He shall be like a tree planted by the rivers of waters" (Ps. 1:3).

Meditation paves the way for divine direction. "Trust in the Lord with all thine heart; and lean not unto thine own understanding. In all thy ways acknowledge him, and he shall direct thy paths" (Prov. 3:5–6). Meditation is acknowledging him in all our ways.

Meditation establishes our thoughts. "Commit thy works unto the Lord, and thy thoughts shall be established" (Prov. 6:3).

Meditation will protect and guard our hearts and our minds. "And the peace of God, which passeth all understanding, will keep your hearts and mind through Christ Jesus" (Phil. 4:7).

I commend meditation to you. Meditate upon the Father, the Lord Jesus, *and* the Holy Spirit. Meditate upon what Jesus is to you and what you are in him. Meditate in the quiet place. Meditate by the way. Meditate on him when sleep will not come. Hush your heart to meditate in the noisy crowd.

Be sure that the Lord is thinking of you. "But I am poor and needy; yet the Lord thinketh up on me" (Ps. 40:17). Reciprocate by thinking upon him. "In the multitude of my thoughts with me thy comforts delight my soul" (Ps. 94:19). "My meditation of him shall be sweet: I will be glad in the Lord" (Ps. 104:34). "How precious also are thy thoughts unto me, O God! how great is the sum of them! If I should count them, they are more in number than the sand: when I awake, I am still with thee" (Ps. 139:17–18).

The privilege of meditation is among his many gifts to you. Fullness of joy awaits your giving it back to him!

20

The Secret of Praying Through

Importunate praying never faints nor grows weary; it is never discouraged; it never yields to cowardice, but is buoyed up and sustained by a hope that knows no despair, a faith that will not let go. Importunate praying has patience to wait and strength to continue. It never prepares itself to quit praying and declines to rise from its knees till an answer is received (E. M. Bounds). [1]

Though he will not rise and give him, because he is his friend, yet because of his importunity he will rise and give as many as he needeth. And I say unto you, Ask, [keep on asking], and it shall be given you; seek [keep on seeking], and ye shall find; knock [keep on knocking], and it shall be opened to you (Luke 11:8–9).

Sometimes God's answers to prayer are *direct.*
Sometimes God's answers are *different.*
Sometimes God's answers are *delayed.*
Sometimes God's answers are *denied.*
We will not come to know of God's answers in a satisfying way apart from the secret of "praying through." I used to hear that term a great deal more than I do today. In fact as I was growing up I became convinced of the necessity of praying about a matter until I knew I was through. I was "through" in the sense that I had gotten through to God as well as in the sense of being finished with that particular prayer.
We have said that there is a time for praise and thanksgiving.

155

There is a time to ask and receive with a definite transaction. There is a time to fervently intercede. But there is also a time to pray, pray, pray until the answer comes.

The Bible calls this "importunate" praying. The word means "shamelessness." Importunity refuses to be denied. Importunity is convinced that the thing prayed for ought to be had and holds on until it is gotten!

Jesus gives us two illustrations of prayer which give much light on the subject of praying through. In these parables Jesus sets forth the necessity of importunity and persistence in prayer.

The first of these parables is in Luke 11. The Lord tells of a man caught in an emergency. Company comes and he has no bread. He goes to the house of a friend at midnight and requests bread. He is at first refused. Friendship is dismissed as a criterion for giving bread. But what friendship cannot do, importunity does! And that man gets his needs met because of his importunity! And Jesus closes that parable by saying, "You keep on asking, and you will keep on receiving; you keep on seeking, and you will keep on finding; you keep on knocking, and it will keep on being opened to you." Each of these words are in the present tense and should be read in a continuing sense. The issue of the parable is obvious.

The second of these parables featuring importunity is found in Luke 18. "And he spake a parable to this end, that men ought always to pray and not to faint." It is clear that the whole teaching of the parable centers around unceasing prayer. He tells of a crude judge who feared neither God nor man, who was approached by a widow in that city requiring him to avenge her of her adversary. What a sense of propriety, justice, or the work of God and man could not do, that widow's persistence won out over the stubborn atheism of that unjust judge! "Yet because this widow troubleth me, I will avenge her, lest by her continual coming she weary me" (v. 5). Here is the application of that fantastic parable, "AND shall not GOD avenge his own elect, which cry day and night unto him, though he BEAR long with them? I tell you that he will avenge them speedily" (vv. 7–8). If the implication were a faint suggestion it would be encouraging. But here is an outright promise that stubborn, persistent praying moves God into immediate action!

While there are times when a thing can be had by simply believing and claiming, there are other times when importunity alone will do the job.

Another clear case of persistence and its payoff is given in Matthew 15. A woman from Canaan came to Jesus with an urgent need. "Have mercy on me, O Lord, thou son of David; my daughter is grievously vexed with a devil." The response of Jesus is puzzling. "He answered her not a word." She kept on crying. The disciples tried to send her away but she persisted. Jesus said, "I am not sent but to the lost sheep of the house of Israel." She stubbornly persisted, "Saying, Lord, help me." He said again, "It is not meet to take the children's bread, and to cast it to dogs." [This was a term meaning "puppies," not "dogs" in the harsh sense.] She came right back, "Yet the dogs eat of the crumbs that fall from their master's table." And friend, at that moment he turned to her and said, "O woman, great is thy faith: be it unto thee even as thou wilt, and her daughter was made whole from that very hour" (vv. 22–28).

Oh, Lord, teach us that kind of prayer that refuses to be denied. This is the kind of prayer that Jesus prayed in the garden. "And he . . . again prayed the third time, saying the same words" (Matt. 26:44). He stayed with it until he had an answer.

Paul knew the value of importunate prayer when he prayed regarding the thorn in his flesh in 2 Corinthians 12. He prayed three times that it might depart from him. There is evidence that the term *three times* may have suggested continuous prayer over a period of time. He was stubborn. God then answered. He had already given Paul all he needed and that was sufficient. Paul had an answer better than the one for which he had prayed! And his persistence paved the way to praise. "Most gladly therefore will I rather glory in my infirmities, that the power of Christ may rest upon me. Therefore I take pleasure in infirmities, in reproaches, in necessities, in persecutions, in distresses for Christ's sake: for when I am weak, then I am strong" (2 Cor. 12:9–10).

Moses refused to be denied and God changed his mind about judgment upon the children of Israel (Num. 14:11–20).

Elijah prayed for rain and sent his servant to investigate. The servant said, "There is nothing." He was told to go again seven times. On the seventh viewing there arose a cloud. Rain was on the way. Elijah had prayed through! (1 Kings 18:41–44).

The imperative necessity of importunate prayer is plainly set forth in the Word of God. It needs to be stated and restated today. We are apt to overlook it even more so today with all of our comforts and ease. Yet, it is a necessity for this surfeited age.

Oh, dear friend let us learn to pray through. Let us not begin to pray and pray a little while and then give it up. Let us pray prevailingly, audaciously, stubbornly. Remember, God told Moses, "Let me alone." Moses refused and God relented. Let us not leave God alone. Let us assault the throne of heaven with holy boldness crying, *O Lord, revive thy work in the midst of the years; in the midst of the years make known; in wrath remember mercy. Oh, that thou wouldst rend the heavens and come down. Revive us again that thy people may rejoice in thee! We refuse to be denied. We call you to remember your promises of old!* (see Hab. 3:2; Isa. 64:1).

But how will we know when we have "prayed through." I can answer that only in this way. We will know! We will not likely know why or how we know, but we will know. Revelation doesn't have to think, it knows. It needs no certification on the sense side, it just knows! The answer will at last have come to the heart and the heart will say, "I have it!"

May God move us today to know experientially the meaning of praying through!

---

1. *Necessity of Prayer, op. cit.*, p. 73.

21
Books on Prayer That Have Most Blessed My Life

I recommend continuous reading on the subject of prayer, biographies of great men of prayer, and repeated reading of certain prayer classics such as some to be mentioned in this following discussion. But with your reading, pray! *Let nothing substitute for prayer and when that which is designed to motivate prayer begins to hinder prayer, drop it and* pray!

I come to the close of this volume at the same point where I began with the fervent invitation for you to come with me to Prayer—Life's Limitless Reach (J.R.T.)

Let us therefore come boldly unto the throne of grace, that we may obtain mercy, and find grace to help in time of need (Heb. 4:16).

For several years I have made it a habit to be reading most all the time a good book on prayer. I have a habit of looking through pastor's studies to see if there is one I have missed. I would recommend to every believer the habit of reading great classics on prayer. This should never be *instead* of the Word of God but *along with* the Word of God. The Bible is transcendingly the greatest book on the vitality of prayer ever written!

To do what I have assigned myself to do is not an easy task but I am impelled to try. The reader will invariably say, "What about this volume or that volume" I am bound to say, if I were to hear you, "Yes, you are right and that one should be added to the top ten." We would soon have a hundred in the top ten!

To my place of prayer I always bring three books, the Bible, my

159

prayer book (which we have already discussed), and a copy of *My Utmost for His Highest* by Oswald Chambers. There has been no book aside from the Bible which has blessed me on a continuous basis in prayer as this one! Miss Bertha Smith has used it for years and continues to use it. I heard her say recently that many times she had sought to use another devotional book but returned to this one because in comparison they all seemed "flat."

I am going to discuss the ten books which have blessed me most on the subject of prayer. You will notice the wording of that statement. I have not made the claim that they are the best books on the subject. They are the ones which have most blessed me. Others have blessed me much and to redeem myself in your estimation I shall list a good many more when I am through discussing these ten!

1. *With Christ in the School of Prayer* by Andrew Murray. This is a leading classic on the subject of prayer. One cannot retain a casual commitment to prayer with the reading of this volume. Walter Barlow writes in the Introduction of an experience when he had the privilege of hearing Andrew Murray speak. He says, "When the company was assembled, Dr. Murray quietly said, 'Let us pray.' The benediction of that prayer abides. We all knew before we met him that he was a religious writer of world renown, as well as South Africa's best beloved preacher. After that prayer we knew we were in the presence of a man of God."

It is a book of thirty-one brief and readable chapters. Each chapter ends with a moving, anointed prayer that lifts the reader up to the throne. All the chapters are great but I have found the following especially helpful: (Each chapter has a double title) Chapter 4, "After This Manner Pray or The Model Prayer": chapter 5, "Ask, and It Shall Be Given You or The Certainty of the Answer to Prayer"; chapter 11 "Believe that Ye Have Received or The Faith That Takes"; chapter 21 "If Ye Abide In Me or The All-Inclusive Condition"; chapter 27 "Father, I will or Christ the High Priest" (based on John 17); and chapter 31 "Pray Without Ceasing or A Life of Prayer." (This is a very brief but powerful chapter on what comprises a life that can pray.)

This volume closes with an epilogue on George Müller and the secret of his power in prayer, a fitting tribute of one great man of prayer to another.

2. *The Kneeling Christian* by An Unknown Christian. This is another great book on prayer. It was first printed by Zondervan over thirty years ago. It is one of several by the Unknown Christian. It is difficult to pick out chapters which are better than others. He begins with a chapter on the necessity of intercession. There is a very skillful and helpful use of illustrations of answered prayer in the book. This 125-page book covers such vital topics as "What Is Prayer?" "How Shall I Pray?" "Must I Agonize?" "Does God Always Answer Prayer?" "How Does God Answer Prayer?" and "Who May Pray?"

In the chapter, "What Is Prayer?" he tells of Moody in one of his meetings asking the question that titled the chapter. The answer received was from a lad, "Prayer is an offering up of our desires to God for things agreeable to his will, in the name of Christ, with confession of our sins and thankful acknowledgement of His mercies." A great definition!

This book will be a thrilling experience to read. I commend it to you.

3. *Destined For the Throne* by Paul E. Billheimer. This book captured my attention as few books ever have! I have read it and reread it! I find it more thrilling the last time than the first. Its full title is astounding and revealing, *A Study in Biblical Cosmology Setting Forth the Ultimate Goal of the Universe Which is the Church Reigning with Christ with a New View of Prayer as On The Job Training in Preparation for the Throne.*

This book bears a 1975 copyright and had just a few weeks ago fallen into my hands. I shall read it again and again. Billy Graham has written in the Foreword, "Every Christian who feels impelled to find a deeper dimension of Christian witness not only should read this book but also study it prayerfully, and apply its principles to his life."

I have drawn extensively from this volume, especially in the discussion on prayer as warfare in chapter 5. This is the freshest and most delightful work on prayer that I have seen in many years. I predict for it a wide and blessed reading.

Each chapter ends with a good many detailed notes that are as helpful as the chapters themselves. Here is a book on philosophy, cosmology, history, and theology with an interpretation that is both shocking and undeniable! He frequently quotes such stalwarts as Wesley, Moody, and Bounds but keeps to his subject of prayer as the key to the universe and history. His respect for the church is refreshing. He says, "God *proposes* . . . a Holy church *disposes*." He pictures the church, as weak as she might seem, administering the decisions already passed upon by God and enforcing them against the gates of hell. He says in the introduction, "In spite of all her lamentable weaknesses, appalling failures, and indefensible shortcomings, the Church is the mightiest force for civilization and enlightened social consciousness in the world today."

Especially helpful is chapter 3 in which he discusses "The Mystery of Prayer" and under that title such topics as ''God, helpless without a man''; "God deputizes his church"; "Prayer . . . on-the-job training for sovereignty"; and "Prayer, the main business of the church."

Another helpful chapter is ''The Problem of Faith." He exclaims in the beginning of the chapter, "The problem of a living faith, of faith without doubt, is a very real one. . . . Large segments of the Body of Christ are baffled by this plague." Then he gives the answer in one word, *praise*. He then speaks of praise for the remainder of the chapter with helpful discussions such as "Why is praise so effective against Satan?" "Praise as a way of life"; "Praise for all things"; "The basis for unceasing praise"; and "Praise, the secret of faith without doubt."

In the final chapter, "Organized Action," he suggests the priority of prayer in both individual and church. He gives some helpful hints as to promoting prayer in the church. In the beginning of the book he candidly makes this statement, "Any church which does not have a well-organized prayer program is simply operating a religious treadmill!"

His last, fitting statement in chapter 9 is "Prayer is where the action is; therefore, Mobilize for prayer!"

4. *The Cycle of Prayer* by Ralph Herring. A friend who knew that I was working on a book on the subject of prayer has loaned me his copy of this book with the claim that it is the greatest book on prayer he has ever read. I now see why he makes that claim. The book is only 80 pages in length but presents a perspective of prayer which is bound to enhance the reader's prayer life. The book is out of print and for this reason I have included in chapter 6 of this volume a summary of *The Cycle of Prayer*. (See note at opening of chap. 6.)

5. *If Ye Shall Ask* by Oswald Chambers. When you meet a work of Oswald Chambers, you can be certain that it is well done! This is no

exception. Any one of several chapters would make the purchase of the book a bargain. An interesting outline begins the first chapter, "What's the Good of Prayer?"

> BECAUSE WE NEED TO.
> > For human wits have an end.
> > For human wills have an end.
> > For human wisdom has an end.
>
> BECAUSE WE MUST DO.
> > If we would know God.
> > If we would help man.
> > If we would do God's will.
>
> BECAUSE WE CAN DO.
> > By asking.
> > By seeking.
> > By knocking.

The whole book is worth the price of the fifth chapter alone. It is entitled "After God's Silence . . . What?" With the reading of this chapter, the reader will be delighted with the prospects of the silences of God. The story used to illustrate the truths of this chapter is that of the raising of Lazarus.

Chapter 7, "Praying in the Holy Ghost," is especially enlightening. He says, "Praying in the Holy Ghost means the power given us by God to maintain a simple relationship to Jesus Christ, and it is most difficult to realize this simple relationship in the matter of prayer."

6. *The Path of Prayer* by Samuel Chadwick. This book was a gift to me by Leonard Ravenhill, the great revivalist and author. I agree with him that it is one of the greatest books on prayer that I have ever read.

No one can match the incomparable style of writing with which Chadwick presents his case for prayer.

An early chapter deals with "Praying in Secret." He says, "If prayer is the greatest achievement on earth, we may be sure that it will call for a discipline that corresponds to its power."

Chapter 5 is powerful, "The Word of God and Prayer." In it he suggests the right devotional use of the Bible. His treatment of "How to Use the Word in Prayer" is unparalleled as far as I am concerned.

Other great chapters are "Praying in the Spirit" and "The Problem of Unanswered Prayer."

7. *The Practice of Prayer* by G. Campbell Morgan (Baker Book

House). If you know of the works of G. Campbell Morgan you do not have to be convinced of the worth of this volume. It will suffice to list the chapter headings:

    I. Preliminary
   II. The Possibility of Prayer
  III. The Platform of Prayer
  IV. The Preparation for Prayer
   V. The Plane of Prayer:
       (a) The Purposes of God
  VI. The Plane of Prayer
       (b) The Pilgrimage of Man
 VII. The Practice of Prayer

Reading, teaching, and putting into practice the principles of this book will lead you to new heights in Christian living.

8. *Prayer* by O. Hallesby. This is indeed a classic on prayer by a man who was one of Norway's leading Christian teachers and writers. He was a seminary professor in Oslo until his death in 1951. His book was first published more than forty-five years ago and continues to be widely read. It is simple and arresting with very little about prayer that the reader has not known at least in part. But he has the ability to couch prayer in a new setting as to give it excitement and appeal. It is a thoroughly scriptural book full of quotable quotes.

9. *Quiet Talks on Prayer* by S. D. Gordon. In the opening chapter he asserts, "The greatest thing anyone can do for God and for man is to pray. It is not the only thing but it is the chief thing. A correct balancing of the possible powers one may exert puts it first."

As few others he deals with the warfare aspect of prayer in the first chapter with such paragraphs as "Prayer, the Deciding Factor in Spiritual Conflict" and "The Earth, the Battlefield of Prayer."

He has a helpful treatment of the subject, "Why the Results are Delayed" (chap. 2). A very strategic chapter contains word of "The Great Outside Hindrance," a discussion of Satan as the enemy of prayer with the power to hold prayer's answer back for a while. He says, "The real pitch of prayer therefore is Satanward!"

A unique treatment of the listening side of prayer is found in chapter 3.

10. *In His Presence* by E. W. Kenyon. The subtitles of this volume reveal its intriguing contents: "The Secret of Prayer," "A Revelation

of What We Are in Christ," "A Solution of the Prayer Problem," and "A New Conception of This Sacred Privilege." One of the unique qualities of Kenyon as a writer is that of the brevity of his paragraphs. When you read his works you will know why the paragraphs are so short. As brief as they are, they speak volumes. If they were longer, you would soon be foundered by too much mental and spiritual food to digest.

He speaks of what prayer is, the prayer habit, how faith is built, and enemies of prayer. If you practice underlining you will be worn out trying to decide what *not* to underline. Every statement is pungent and powerful.

His chapter on "Prayer and the Church" is fantastic.

Now, my ten is up and I am almost certain that my reader, if he has read much in the field of prayer, would vote for having me boiled in oil for leaving out E. M. Bounds! My problem was, I simply didn't know where to put him!

So to redeem myself, I am recommending:

A Treasury of Prayer by Leonard Ravenhill which is a combination of the seven books by E. M. Bounds on prayer. You see, if I had listed the seven (which I would have in regard to their value), I would have had no room for the others. Several of these volumes by Bounds, long out of print, are being reprinted. I am glad! They are: *Power Through Prayer, Purpose in Prayer, The Necessity of Prayer, The Essentials of Prayer, The Weapon of Prayer, The Possibilities of Prayer, The Reality of Prayer.*

Other great books on prayer are:

The Power of Positive Praying by John Bisagno (Zondervan)
Seven Wonders of Prayer by Armin Gesswein (Zondervan)
A Practical Primer on Prayer by Dorothy Haskin (Moody Press)
Successful Praying by F. J. Huegel (Dimension Books)
Always in Prayer by E. F. Hallock (Hallock)
Prevailing Prayer by D. L. Moody (Moody Press)
Prevailing Prayer by Charles G. Finney (Kregel)
How to Pray by R. A. Torrey (Moody Press)
The Power of Prayer by R. A. Torrey (Moody Press)
Why God Used D. L. Moody by R. A. Torrey (Moody Press)
Prayer . . . Asking and Receiving by John R. Rice (Sword of the Lord)
Pray in the Spirit by Arthur Wallis (Christian Literature Crusade)
Lord, Teach Us to Pray by Alexander Whyte (Hodder and Stoughton)

The Prayer Life by Andrew Murray (Moody Press)
Waiting on God by Andrew Murray (Moody Press)
The Mission of and Praying in the Holy Ghost by H A. Ironside
    (Loizeaux Brother, Inc.)

These are only a few of many volumes on the inexhaustible subject
of prayer.

If I have left off your favorite, write it in and let me know so I can list
it next time!

Happy reading and happy praying!

Bibliography

BILLHEIMER, PAUL E. *Destined for the Throne*. Fort Washington, Pa.: 1975.

BISAGNO, JOHN. *The Power of Positive Praying*. Grand Rapids: Zondervan Publishing House, 1965.

BOUNDS, E. M. *The Reality of Prayer*. Zondervan Publishing House, Grand Rapids, 1962.

⸻. *The Necessity of Prayer*. Grand Rapids: Baker Book House, 1976.

⸻. *Power Through Prayer*. Grand Rapids: Zondervan Publishing House, 1962.

BUNYAN, JOHN. *Prayer*. London: The Banner of Truth Trust, 1965.

CHADWICK, SAMUEL. *The Path of Prayer*. Liverpool, London, and Prescott, 1931.

CHAMBERS, OSWALD. *My Utmost for His Highest*. Toronto: Dodd, Mead, and Company, 1935.

⸻. *If Ye Shall Ask*. Alexandria, La.: Lamplighter Publishers.

DEMARAY, DONALD E. *Alive to God Through Prayer*. Grand Rapids: Baker Book House, 1965.

EPP, THEODORE. *Praying with Authority*. Lincoln, N. C.: Back to the Bible Broadcast, 1965.

FINNEY, CHARLES G. *Prevailing Prayer*. Grand Rapids: Kregel Publications, 1965.

GESSWEIN, ARMIN R. *Seven Wonders of Prayer*. Grand Rapids: Zondervan Publishing House, 1957.

GORDON, S. D. *Quiet Talks on Prayer*. New York: Pyramid Publications. 1967.

GUTZKE, MANFORD. *Plain Talk on Prayer*. Grand Rapids: Baker Book House, 1973.

HALLESBY, O. *Prayer*. Minneapolis, Minn.: Augsburg Publishing House, 1931 (renewed, 1959).

HALLOCK, E. F. *Always in Prayer*. Nashville: Broadman Press, 1966. Later published by author, Norman, Okla.

HARVEY, EDWIN AND LILLIAN. *Kneeling We Triumph*. Chicago: Moody Press, 1971.

HASKIN, DOROTHY. *A Practical Primer on Prayer*. Chicago: Moody Press, 1951.

HERRING, RALPH. *The Cycle of Prayer*. Nashville: Broadman Press, 1966; Wheaton: Tyndale House Publishers, 1974.

HUEGEL, F. J. *Successful Praying*. Minneapolis, Minn.: Dimensions Books, Bethany Fellowship, Inc., 1967.

———. *The Ministry of Intercession*. Minneapolis, Minn.: Dimensions Books, Bethany Fellowship, Inc., 1967.

IRONSIDE, H. A. *The Mission of and Praying in the Holy Spirit*. Neptune, N. J.: Loizeaux Brothers, Inc., 1957.

KENYON, E. W. *In His Presence*. Seattle: Kenyon Publishing Co., 1969.

———. *The Wonderful Name of Jesus*. Seattle: Kenyon Publishing Co., 1964.

KING, GEOFFREY. *Let Us Pray*. Fort Washington, Pa.: Christian Literature Crusade.

LAUBACH, FRANK. *Prayer . . . The Mightiest Force in the World*. Westwood, N. J., Spire Books, Fleming H. Revell, 1946.

LOCKYER, HERBERT. *How I Can Make Prayer More Effective*. Edinburgh: Marshall, Morgan, and Scott, 1953.

McCONKEY, JAMES. *Prayer*. Wrightsville, Pa.: Silver Publishers Society, 1905.

MOODY, D. L. *Prevailing Prayer*. Chicago: Moody Press.

MORGAN, G. CAMPBELL. *The Practice of Prayer*. Alexandria, La.: Lamplighter Publications.

RAVENHILL, LEONARD. *A Treasury of Prayer*. Zachery, La.: Fires of Revival Publishers, 1961.